Success is No Fluke

— A complete book on personality development

Lt Col RK Langar (Retd.)

Vitasta

Vitasta Publishing Pvt. Ltd.
New Delhi

Published by
Renu Kaul Verma for
Vitasta Publishing Pvt. Ltd.
2/15, Ansari Road, Daryaganj,
New Delhi - 110 002

ISBN 978-81-89766-84-9

Cover Design and Layout by Vitasta Publishing Pvt. Ltd.
Printed by Vits Press, New Delhi

Success is No Fluke

— A complete book on personality development

Dedication

To my wife SUSHMA

Who put me on the spiritual path and made me understand the spiritual truths. Her memory inspires me to contribute towards the well-being of society through my writings and talks.

Contents

Acknowledgements

To my daughter Dr Sonali Langar for her valuable suggestions in giving practical shape to my ideas while working on the book. Her deep interest in my work enthused me to work on the book in a purposeful manner.

To my son-in-law Dr Vinay Bhat for sparing his valuable time in assisting me more than one way at different stages of compilation of the material presented in the book.

To my granddaughter Radha who has arrived in the world recently, for her divine presence which stimulates my thoughts.

To Mr Sudesh K Verma—Managing Director of Vitasta Publishing Pvt Ltd, New Delhi—who advised me about the contents and chapterization. His suggestions on improvement added immense value to this book.

To Ms Anuradha who was involved in the editing process of the book from its very inception.

To Gurvinder Chhatwal (Binny) for his invaluable help given to me while working on this book.

Acknowledgements

Preface

It gives me immense satisfaction to write *Success is No Fluke.* Everyone wants to be successful in life but real success lies in the development of one's personality with a spiritual blend. I have put across my views on the essence of spirituality and its role in developing a wholesome personality. The book aims at promoting spiritual and moral values of life which are found wanting in present times.

The book intends to engage in conversation with a common man who aspires to achieve big but tries to find meaning when he is showered with repeated failures despite best endeavours. I have tried to present the rudiments of Indian cultural and spiritual thoughts. These will be of interest to those who want to understand the cultural values that have inspired success and encouraged people to rise despite failures. The book will be specifically beneficial to students and teaching community. The book is written with a view to provide spiritual counselling to enhance psychological growth for attaining psychosocial development of society. As a writer, my aim is to help readers to understand our value system.

Today's learning is oriented to earning which is a very limited view of learning and knowledge. LEARNING TO BE is far more important than LEARNING TO EARN.

Are You Fishing for a Compliment?

Do not hand over remote of yours in others' hands.

Sri Sri Ravi Shankar

Are you fishing for a compliment? Most of us would be shy of answering a straight question like this in public. The answer would in all probability be a big NO. Allow the ego curtain to fall, and most of us would concede that we do look for compliments of those around us for everything we do. There is no denying the fact that we always wish to be recognized and lauded. There are times when we are unsure about how good we are, yet, we want others to appreciate the goodness of our heart.

My daughter, when she was a child, often asked me, "Papa, am I looking beautiful?" My one statement, "Yes darling, you are," would make her immensely happy and confident. The best way to make her dress well for parties was to tell her that she was not looking okay and she would at once change into the right kind of clothes.

This holds true for all of us. We all try to see a Shahrukh Khan or a Sachin Tendulkar in ourselves. We are all trying to do something meaningful and we want others to recognize our efforts.

This phenomenon is all-pervasive and is observed at the spiritual level too. I have seen many spiritual leaders expecting their disciples to tell them that they are the best in the field. Thus, we see that there is always a temptation to extract appreciation from others. This is inculcated through the Looking-Glass Self socialization by which a person looks into the eyes of others as he would do in the mirror and tries to find out the reactions his actions produce on others. Although this happens more during childhood, one does not get cured of it even during adulthood.

Why do we want people to compliment us? Is it because we are not sure about ourselves, or is it because we are lacking something in our personality? Do we wish to use others' appreciation to make up for the deficiency? It could be that we want fame which compels us to order our life on favourable opinion of others about us. And in order to get appreciation from others, we may do certain things which are not in tune with our natural disposition. When that happens, we are likely to become artificial or unnatural and move away from our true state of existence. On the other hand, when we are genuinely good and we know that we are moving along the righteous path, we remain established in our goodness, whatever the outer conditions may be. We then do not require any certificate from others to proclaim our goodness. In any case, people will acknowledge our goodness sooner or later. While it is true that some of us may need appreciation to motivate us to do better, it should not unduly prompt us to make it a habit to shape our life on the opinion of others. We should not go out of the way to receive appreciation from others. At times, our desire to act as per wishes of others lands us in ludicrous situations, where we make ourselves a laughing stock.

We should follow Gautam Buddha's advice which he gave to mankind more than 2,500 years ago. He said, "Be good and do good." If we are genuinely good and do acts with good intentions, the world would notice us automatically. The way a deer cannot hide its *kasturi* (fragrance of musk), goodness cannot remain hidden from others. The other thing is that when we are good and when we are convinced about our goodness, we are sure of where we stand because all our actions are anchored on righteousness. We are not disturbed by any unhealthy remarks of others about us. Not only that, we do not accept any ill opinion of others directed on us.

There is a beautiful episode from the life of Gautam Buddha to illustrate how a good person should respond towards the ill deeds of others. Once Buddha went out begging for food along with his disciple Ananda. Buddha stopped at a house and asked the lady of the house to give him food. The lady refused, saying that Buddha was a healthy person and should earn his living instead of begging from others. Buddha being a monk was required to beg for his food as per the traditions of monks. Therefore, he insisted that he should be given food. The lady got annoyed on his insistence and brought all the filth of the house and placed it in his begging bowl. Ananda got furious to see his master being insulted but Buddha remained calm. He told Ananda that he does not accept what the lady wanted to give him and the matter ends there. He further clarified that if he gave Ananda a book and if the book is not accepted by him, then the book will come back to Buddha. Similarly, he did not accept the rubbish which the lady wanted to give him; the rubbish would go back to the lady. Buddha was so sure about his goodness and righteousness that he was not disturbed by the unruly behaviour of the lady.

The moral of the story is that when we are convinced that we are on the righteous path, we take no notice of what people tell us or think of us. Then we are not agitated or troubled by harsh conduct of others directed towards us. We simply refuse to be guided by such behavioural patterns. When we know we are good, we do not bother about compliments of others. It is a different thing if people praise us on their own. In that case, we need to accept it thankfully with generosity. Lord Krishna says in the *Bhagavad Gita* that he is dear to Him who is not troubled by others because he knows that he is established in truth, having risen above both good and bad.

One thing I have noticed that if you ask someone if he or she is good, the reply which comes out invariably is 'I do not know, ask others what they feel about me.' This is relying on others to call yourself good and not having your own conviction about it. Why should we ask others about our own goodness when we know unmistakably that we are good? One should have one's own conviction about it. There may be an element of modesty in the reply but still people should know themselves well. Why should we pass on the baton of judging us to others? Our instant answer should be, 'Yes I am good.' It should rest on the person asking the question to make his independent assessment.

When we are young, our parents often praise us for our behaviour and we feel elevated to hear good remarks because children expect others to tell them so. But when we grow up, we should not wait for people to tell us how good we are. When we order our life on the opinion of others, we make no effort to raise ourselves or develop our personality. Therefore, we must take charge of our life and evolve ourselves to acquire a wholesome personality with self-effort and without being dependent on others.

Sociologist CH Cooley described this propensity to look into the eyes of others to know oneself as the Looking-Glass Self. In the process of socialization, a child learns to grow in the perception of others. He knows when his parents like him and behaves accordingly to get appreciation. By doing so, he starts developing his own personality. A child first imagines how he must appear to others before he experiences the judgment of others. He develops his self through the judgment of others. In interactions with his significant others and peer groups, he begins to develop an identity of his own. But this process is okay for growing children. Once the consciousness about the self is developed, the person needs to graduate to forming his own opinion about good and bad. This would come with the development of the self. Abraham Lincoln said that great men don't follow society, society follows them. The *Bhagavad Gita*, which has an honoured place in world literature, also speaks in the same voice. It says that whatsoever a great man does, the same is done by others. Whatever standards he sets the world follows. It says great men are pathmakers.

But who are these great men? Are they born great? Great men are those who discover the right way, walk it and reach their goal of life. They choose their own direction in life. They believe that human nature is ever changing and not fixed, and hence can be transformed. They go beyond their own self after knowing first what they are. They believe that self-awareness is a means of self-improvement. Great men are those who do not believe in destiny. They design it themselves by developing their personality. They are successful leaders. But why is it that great men are few and not many? The reason is that majority of men have no conviction of their own and follow the society. It is rightly said that few find the right way and still fewer walk it. Fewer are still who enter into real life. Fewer again are those who reach the goal. People know what the right path is but still they are tempted to take the wrong path because it requires no personal effort for taking the wrong way. Duryodhana, a key figure in the *Mahabharata* complains, "I know what is good and what is evil but the problem is I possess neither the desire to do good nor the restraint to stop doing evil." How true is this statement? What it amounts to is that degrading oneself is an easier path than elevating oneself.

The purpose of life is to attain spiritual elevation. One must rise above the self and try to achieve the highest in oneself. Only then we can work without bothering about criticisms of others. Abraham Maslow called it an attempt to achieve self-actualization. The father of humanistic behavioural psychology, Maslow said that man's highest needs are spiritual. Using psychology, he tried to analyse human behaviour. The deeper one goes within oneself, the more he knows about human nature, he said and termed this process of knowing oneself as 'self-actualization'. He analysed different motivations that guide human behaviour at different stages. One who is hungry would be guided by the need to satiate hunger and one whose belly is full would be guided by other needs that are needed after food. But there are some who are inspired by the need of self-actualization. Mahatma Gandhi was one who could go to any extent to be of service to the needy. He was definitely guided by the highest order need of achieving the best in a human being. He was not much bothered about what people thought about him and he was always inspired by his self-righteousness.

A distinguished human being speaks in relation to his particular attainment or the height which he has attained. The meaning of what he says may not always be immediately known but what he says and what he has attained is real. Then what a man thinks cannot be separated from what he is. Self-actualization would mean connecting with the self, the deeper inside us that is different from non-self or the matter. When you are absorbed in self or the spirit within, you are more and more conscious about yourself. On the other hand, when one is absorbed in non-self or matter, one tends to become less conscious of himself. Then one becomes less self-aware, less apt to observe oneself as spectator, less self-criticizing, self-evaluating, self-selecting and rejecting, and less self-judging. All these inner activities come in the forefront when one is not connected with the deep inside himself.

Let us try to understand what a self-actualized person is. Self-actualization is making choices and being honest when in doubt rather than not. Self-actualized people are involved in a cause outside their own, in something outside of them. It is finding out who one is and what his tastes are, what is good as well as bad for him. Self-actualized people have a feeling of security and they feel safe when they are in contact with fellow beings. They have adequate self-esteem and a feeling of self-value proportionate to their individual achievements. Hence, a self-actualized personality is one that reflects on personal growth and development in daily life. Self-actualization tilts the mind towards spirituality. It is the beginning of spirituality since finding out the best in oneself is the path to discover God and all good qualities associated with Him.

It would be appropriate to name here some of the world's greatest men who became great because of their single pursuit of excellence or the highest in the vocation they chose. George Washington, the founding father and the first President of the United States of America, was honest to the core and never used the physical power under his command for any self-gain. He was basically a good human being—first in war, first in peace and first in the hearts of his countrymen. Napoleon Bonaparte dared where nobody else could. He conquered a vast territory by sheer reliance on his own self. The term Napoleonic is used to compare any person who has the charismatic characteristics of determination and will. Mahatma Gandhi was always in search of the highest possible in him. Only a person in search of truth could decide to live half-naked till the countrymen were poor. He left everything in order to identify with the Indian masses and to get the country rid of foreign rule. He was a true mass leader who swayed people along with him. Gandhiji's disciple Jawaharlal Nehru was determined to make India modern. His single-minded determination resulted into India emerging as an industrialized nation. Ram Manohar Lohia—who presented an understandable form of socialism, quite different from the concepts of Hegel, Marx and Lenin—was a self-actualized person of a very high order. He lent his voice for uplift of the lower castes of India. He said, "Many socialists honestly but wrongly think that it is sufficient to strive for economic equality and caste inequality will vanish of itself as a consequence. They fail to comprehend that economic inequality and caste inequality are twin demons which have both to be killed." More than a century ago, Swami Vivekananda said that weaker castes should be given more than higher castes to bring them at par with the latter. Then only the inequality of castes will disappear.

In spiritual terminology, self-actualization could be referred to as self-realization or self-fulfilment which is development of full potential of something in us through different facets of Yoga. If something is fulfilled, it is completed or it has been actualized. Synonym of self-fulfilment is self-realization or completion. By self-fulfilment we mean a smooth and joyful life leading to permanent bliss or *ananda*. Spirituality, which is the bedrock of Indian culture, plays an extremely important role in developing our personality. It is a means of achieving human excellence as spiritual awakening gives power, glory, fortune and purity. Everything that is excellent will come when we raise ourselves to the level of divinity within us which is our soul, the very essence of human being. What is referred to as self-confidence or self-reliance is believing in the glory of one's own self. Happiness, what is sought after by each and every individual, is permanently obtained when we raise ourselves to our spiritual level. Happiness, whose Sanskrit equivalent is *sukham,* is synonymous with joy which is generally associated with sense enjoyments. For example, fulfilment of our desire for health, money, appreciation and position does give us happiness but it is not total and all inclusive. True happiness is not joy but bliss or *ananda*. This is not sense enjoyment but is super sensuous joy. Bliss is a state which is beyond both happiness and suffering. As per Indian philosophy, the world is a pair of opposite. For example, darkness and light, and enjoyment and suffering belong to the pair of opposites. The realization that happiness and sorrow are only two sides of the same coin will eventually enable man to go beyond both and attain transcendental bliss or true happiness. For example, peace is neither enjoyment nor suffering. Peace is a state of bliss. To obtain peace one cannot be at war with others. Happiness does not mean you wait for completion of big things in order to obtain it. You should look for happiness while indulging in small things and you would invariably find it.

Importance of Attitude

A spiritual outlook changes our attitude towards life. Attitude becomes firm when we start thinking about different aspects of life, when we look for an out of the box solution to our problems. Man's success in life depends upon hard work, sincerity, honesty, faith in oneself, commitment, transparency and, most importantly, his attitude towards life. Attitude is the mother of all values and positivity is the harvest of attitude. A man may be born ordinary but he does something extraordinary when he develops an attitude to become good and do good. At the spiritual level, we develop an attitude that makes us see the brighter side of things.

Mata Amritanandamayi Devi, popularly called *Amma* (Mother), is one of India's most celebrated spiritual guides. She says it is the right attitude that would free us from all limitations. Attitude moulds aptitude. Harvard University research indicates that in achieving success only 15 per cent is contributed by information and the balance 85 per cent is contributed by the attitude of a person. Is it not ironical that our modern education is focussed only on facts and figures and not much attention is given to shaping attitude? We should have a never-die attitude because life is not always smooth sailing. It is said that attitude is the difference between the best and You. Our attitude should be to act in the world, as there is no other choice, and do our best to improve it. Every situation is an opportunity for learning and growth. Never say die is what is needed to reach at the top of all endeavour. Attitude should be cooperative and not competitive. One should have 'what can I contribute' attitude towards the world.

One who walks on the spiritual path develops a loving and affectionate relationship with all since he considers others as an extension of his own self. He focusses on the goodness and beauty of others to bring out their hidden talents. But unfortunately, at our ordinary state of existence, our relationship with others gets spoiled since we expect from others to maintain our relationship with them. The more balanced a man is in his relationship with others, the more successful he would be even though he may not possess extraordinary intelligence. We should display a little bit of sensitivity in our relationship. Expectations create dependency more so when we expect from others what we want and which can never be given to us. We find difficulty in living with others because we have expectations from them, and when they fail to satisfy our expectations, we feel frustrated. But this is also a fact of life that when one is living with others, some expectations are bound to arise on the principle of give and take. But too much of expectations create dependency.

Those who depend upon others lead a miserable life, whereas those who are dependent upon by others are assets to the society. Emotional expectation is the worst type of expectation. The beauty of our relationship with others is not to expect anything in return for directing our love and good behaviour towards them. It costs a beautiful person no exertion to paint his image in the eyes of others. Similarly, it costs nothing to a spiritual person to maintain good relationship with others. This is how a spiritually-inclined person would maintain his relationship with others. Whatever he does will create a peaceful, joyful and a loving world around him. He will have the conviction to live exactly how he chooses.

Relationship should be governed by love for others and not on expectations or obligations. Man has infinite capability and potential since he is spiritual at the core. In fact, he is a spark of the Divine power. Man's foremost responsibility is to maintain good relationship with his family members. No matter what you have done for yourself or for humanity, if you cannot give proper attention to your own family members then what have you really accomplished? Sri Sri Ravi Shankar, a spiritual saint and humanitarian par excellence, says that expectation reduces joy even if it is expected to happen. It is not wrong to expect particularly when you are living with others on the basis of give and take but the only problem expectation creates is that it puts us on a wanting mode. Sometimes we may be getting much more from the person we expect, but when we do not get what we want, it makes us unhappy. Wanting always makes us unhappy contrary to giving that contributes towards our happiness.

It should be clearly understood that relationships should never be taken for granted. A little formality is essential in all relationships including that between husband and wife. What is required is to unlock our divine potential by aligning oneself to a higher ideal. Higher the ideal, the greater will a man acquire the ability to work for the good of others. Spirituality blends us into a wholesome being where we consider self-help as the best help. We learn to stand on our own feet without depending on others. A spiritual disposition gives comfort to those who come in our contact. A spiritual person is like a peepul tree that gives shelter to all; he is an ambassador of peace and harmony with a passion to serve the humanity. Smell of flower goes in the direction of the wind but goodness of a spiritually-elevated person goes in all directions, even against the direction of the wind. He looks for good in every situation. He believes that self-transformation is the way to world transformation. To move on the spiritual path, what is required is an inner transformation to rise to a higher state of existence.

Inner Transformation

Inner transformation means changing ourselves from our present state of existence to a higher state. It is based on the assumption that all men are not perfect by birth but can become so with self-effort. Inner transformation presupposes that there is something in a person which needs to be changed for the better. Human nature being a changeable commodity, it can be transformed to a better state with self-effort. The *Bhagavad Gita* says that all undertakings have some defect like smoke in fire. Similarly, all human beings have some negative traits that need to be transformed. It is a different matter that some people realize it while others do not. In the larger sense, inner transformation would mean turning negative emotions such as anger, lust, ego, deceit and falsehood into positive emotions of truth, compassion, peace, forgiveness, humility and simplicity. Inner transformation aims at converting vices into virtues and demerits into merits. It is like going from darkness to light, leading one to live a purposeful existence. Inner transformation means working on one's own self for self-uplift.

Change of Heart

In spiritual language, transformation implies a change of heart—not the physical heart but the conceptual centre in our being from where positive emotions such as love, compassion, sympathy, forgiveness, truthfulness, peace and righteousness are radiated. It is rightly said that one beautiful heart is better than thousand beautiful faces. The innermost part of human personality, the core of human being, the self or the consciousness is ever pure. But at our ordinary state of existence, the pure consciousness within is covered with psychological distortions, comprising mostly our negative instincts. So change of heart will mean change of our negativity into positivity, leading to a behavioural pattern of the individual corresponding to higher values of life. Inner transformation is fighting inner battle of life.

Generally, we are concerned with fighting the outer battle of life where one has to tackle day-to-day problems of worldly existence. But the main battle of life is not the outer one. It is the inner battle where one has to identify inner weaknesses and eliminate them through the process of discrimination. This requires each one of us to set aside some time from our daily routine to look within to find out where we stand in terms of our merits and demerits. This process is called self-examination, self-study or self-introspection. One of the Greek philosophers tells us that an unexamined life is not worth living. Having found our strengths and weaknesses, we should enlarge our strengths to weaken our weaknesses. With constant vigil, concentration and practice, we get into the process of removing our bad habits and undesirable tendencies which automatically strengthens our positive traits. It is no good knowing what is good. There is a need to practise goodness or, as they say living, goodness that really transforms life. While we are engaged in the inner battle of life, we have to keep a check over our thoughts and sentiments so that our outer actions do not cause any impurity within. Self-awareness tells us what we are and how can we uplift ourselves to a higher state.

Aids for Inner Transformation

We should make use of the aids available to us for our inner transformation. These aides include our scriptures which act not only as the perfect guide but also elevate our level of existence. Lives of great men and sages help us to draw our lessons and inspirations. We can choose our role model, which could be a scripture or a human being, and follow it in thoughts, words and deeds. We need an open mind to accept what our role model tells us. Open mind means that we are not coloured by our own views. The *Bhagavad Gita*, which by itself is a perfect role model for self-evolution, says that let the scriptures be your authority in ascertaining what ought to be done and what ought not to be done. Having known what has been prescribed by the scriptures, you should act in this manner. In Christianity, it is believed that God has already planned the process of human transformation and for this purpose God sent His son Jesus Christ to show us the way to God. Jesus said, "Be perfect as your Heavenly Father is perfect." Islam says that God has given man a code of conduct, the right path that frees mankind from all ills and makes life worth living. The *Holy Qur'an* declares about itself, "Here is the book where there is no trace of doubt."

Our Goal and Aim

Aim of each and every religion is to make us a spiritual person, anchored fully on a sound moral base. Indian spiritual tradition says that self-realization is the goal of human life. When understood correctly, religion is the highest motive power capable of injecting higher values of life into us. Sri Aurobindo says that those who choose God are chosen by God and therefore we should not miss any opportunity to seek God through our religion. With God on our side, inner transformation becomes easy. Transformation of the whole man is not isolation of immortal spirit from mortal human life but it is transformation of the whole man. Only when there is inner transformation man realizes that all problems and also their solutions are inside him. Inner transformation is a slow process but no effort is wasted. Inner transformation leads to world transformation. You may be born ordinary in your own eyes, but you are not ordinary since you are divine at the core of your personality. Therefore, do not end life as an ordinary person. Build up your personality. Be not small minded, egoistic and nasty. Accommodate others and contribute towards their well-being. As we raise our state of existence, our concept of happiness also changes. Then we look for true happiness which is not dependent on any external agency.

True Happiness

Most of us derive happiness from fulfilment of desires without realizing that true happiness and desires do not go together. When people obtain worldly things in accordance with their desires and expectations, they feel happy. A hungry person feels happy when he gets food. An unemployed person feels happy when he gets a job. An actor feels happy when people applaud his performance. Even a thief is happy when he is successful in his action. There are others who feel happy when they get money from unexpected quarters. Many of us recognize different forms of happiness but no one has clear notion about it. All these types of happiness are conditional where one has to depend on external world to obtain them, or when we are at the mercy of environment to make us happy.

Environmental-based happiness is never continuous because after getting what we want, we keep our eye on getting something else from the outside world. Alexander the Great,also referred to as the Emperor of the World, conquered huge territory of the globe but died an unhappy man since he was seeking happiness from the outside world. What is the use of world conquest if a man is unable to control himself or find inner peace? Socrates, the Greek philosopher, said that the indispensable condition for happiness is not to have something we badly need. What he wants to convey is that worldly processions do not give the happiness that we are looking for. Not getting what you want is sometimes wonderful because in the long run it proves beneficial. Rich people may not be as happy as we consider them to be because money by itself is not happiness even though money is a means to acquire worldly things that gives us comfort and short-lived pleasures. From worldly things we cannot obtain permanent happiness.

Where do we look for lasting happiness? It is only possible when we truly understand that happiness lies within us but beyond our body level. Senses, mind and intellect are parts of our body and happiness obtained at their level can never be permanent. We cannot obtain permanent happiness from the worldly flow of impermanence. Any amount of pleasure seeking cannot give us happiness in the true sense. When we depend on others for our happiness, it is conditional happiness which disappears when things on which we depend are removed.

Our great sages and seers have dwelt on this and have come to the conclusion that the very nature of our self or *atma* is happiness. We are by nature inclined towards happiness or bliss and not sorrow because bliss is our natural condition and sadness our unnatural condition. Happiness being our innate nature, we need not have any reason to be not happy. On the same count, we shall always need some reason to feel unhappy or sad. A person can stay in his natural state but not in his unnatural state even though sadness is a part of our life. To know our nature, we have to get ourselves established in *atma* or truth and feel the permanent and never-ending bliss which transcends both happiness and sorrow. In this state, our happiness is moral and spiritual which gives us contentment of the highest order. Happiness comes from the sense of satisfaction by doing what is right, by doing good and by helping the needy.

When a person is spiritual and follows the moral principles, he can achieve true happiness. On the contrary, a person who is not spiritually inclined and does not follow moral principles can never be truly happy. A spiritual person is one who lives in harmony with the whole creation. That which is infinite is the cause of true happiness. In the finite, there is no lasting happiness. When a man is happy inwardly, the society in which he lives grows. It can be tested with our experience that the more we care for the happiness of others, happier we become. It is said that happiness and sorrow are within us. If we live rightfully, we are bound to achieve eternal happiness. Such happiness gets manifested when we adopt virtues, lead a simple and sincere life and remain humble under all circumstances.

We should not make happiness a separate goal to be attained in isolation. Happiness is to be made a by-product of living a morally-elevated life having a right and enlightened attitude of life. For real happiness, a man should be complete and have no desires for worldly things. If he nurtures worldly desires then he is incomplete. One major cause of our unhappiness is that we tend to compare ourselves with those who are better placed in life than us. Such comparisons take us nowhere. The golden rule is that on your material gains, look at those who are not as well placed as you and then you will discover that you have enough. While doing so you shall feel contented and satisfied. By all means, for your self-development look up to the company of wise men who are at a better state of existence than you.

Let us see how our scriptures define lasting happiness. The *Bhagavad Gita* describes true happiness as the one gained by long practice of disciplines which is like poison in the beginning but nectar-like in the end. It springs from serenity arising from the consciousness of the *atma* or soul inside us and puts an end to all sorrows. While treading the spiritual path and practising self-restraint, a feeling of physical and mental unrest manifests in the beginning. But this pain and unrest turns into bliss and joy as one advances on the spiritual path. This is what the *Bhagavad Gita* refers to as poison in the beginning but nectar-like in the end. It further describes worldly happiness born of union of senses with their objects. It appears nectar-like in the beginning but turns to poison in the end. In our worldly life, our contact with sense objects is unavoidable. So man has to apply restrain on himself so as not to be lured by them. If at all he has to enjoy contact with sense objects, then it has to be a pure sense enjoyment without any craving or longing for them. This would keep the person unaffected when sense objects are removed. Only an enlightened person can have such experience. It explains that real happiness comes from a peaceful mind and to remain peaceful, one must remain unperturbed while facing the stresses of life. The *Bhagavad Gita* further advises us that we should treat pleasure and pain, gain and loss alike by evolving ourselves into a higher state of existence where we transcend the pairs of the opposites. Happiness has to do more with our attitude and less with the circumstances.

Shankara says that whether one is a *yogi* (spiritual person) or *bhogi* (worldly man), *sanyasi* (who has renounced the world) or *grihasthai* (householder), he alone is truly happy and joyful who is inwardly established in *Brahman* or his real self. The greatest source of happiness lies in remembrance of God. This is perfect and eternal happiness which is all inclusive and not isolated. This is unconditional happiness which lies above and beyond the senses and body. This lasting happiness depends upon what you are and not what you possess.

Buddha said suffering is born out of desires. For eternal peace and happiness, one must overcome desires. When we reach a state where there is no desire, happiness inside us blossoms. This was earlier clouded by our desires in the same manner as clouds cover the sun which when drifts away the sun shines brilliantly. We all know that when our desires are not fulfilled, we remain unhappy. We again become unhappy when things that we expect are not available to us. The ultimate happiness lies in a state when we do not look for a reason to be happy. When we look for a reason to be happy, we shall remain unhappy. It is a time-tested experience that when we give happiness to others we ourselves become happy. It is said that happiness derived from worldly objects is not worth a sixteenth part of what comes from cessation of desires. A person who is good himself does good to others and his mind is ever settled on God is the only one who can get a taste of true unconditional happiness. He lives in the Divine consciousness.

> *Almost every man wastes part of his life in attempts to display qualities which he does not possess, and to gain applause which he cannot keep.*
>
> ***Samuel Johnson***

Spirituality and Personality Development

Human potential is the same for all. Your feeling, "I am of no value", is wrong. Absolutely wrong. You are deceiving yourself. We all have the power of thought—so what are you lacking? If you have willpower, then you can change anything. It is usually said that you are your own master.

Dalai Lama

I have submitted in the previous chapter that when one is good and does not feel the need to fish appreciation from others, one rises above the material aspects of life. One sees oneself as one really is. One becomes spiritual at the core. According to Ralph Emerson, a western philosopher, great men are those who perceive the spiritual force to be stronger than the material force. There are also great people who are convinced that thoughts or ideas rule the world. There could be no better truth than this. A spiritual person has a better understanding of things within and outside. He lives with full consciousness and is, therefore, acutely aware of all that he does. He is not driven by life; he is alert and lives in the present spontaneously. He not only understands human values but lives them too.

Here, it is important to differentiate between spirituality and mysticism. Spirituality is basically an Indian concept whereas mysticism is more of a western idea of spirituality. Mysticism is sometimes defined as occult, with hidden meaning, which at times may be obscure to human understanding. On the other hand, spirituality is the acceptance of man's inner divinity which stands higher to both body and mind while encompassing both at the same time. Earlier, Indian practices were termed as mystical, but now, and very rightly so, these are referred to as spiritual practices which offer a sense of fulfilment and wellness to both body and mind. Indian spirituality is a fact of meaningful existence.. Albert Einstein reinforced this when he said that Indian spirituality begins where science ends. While the West has realized this now, India said the same more than 5,000 years ago through the *Bhagavad Gita*. Treating mind exclusively is a western psychiatric practice whereas Indian spiritual practices look after all four major components of human personality that is body, mind, intellect and soul. We shall now study spirituality and its relationship with religion.

Defining Spirituality

Spirituality is the backbone of Indian philosophy or we can rather say that Indian philosophy is eclipsed by Indian spirituality. It aims at living life in the highest consciousness and involving maximum awareness. Spirituality aims at recognizing the divine principle in a man and growing with that principle to bring about harmony and freedom in man's inner and outer life. When we grow spiritually, we also maintain healthy relationship with others. Spirituality is the knowledge and realization of the fact that our soul is divine in nature being a fraction of God and that it is the same soul which exists in all beings. In its absolute sense, spirituality is that illumined state of existence which one attains after realizing one's identity with God. Spirituality is an upward movement which recognizes that God is present in all forms. Indian philosophical thought gives a practical way of reaching to the Supreme. If a man is a part of the Divine, he must become aware of his true nature. In its relative sense, spirituality means living a noble life anchored on the moral values which could ultimately lead us to God or self-realization.

Spirituality is the realization that man is not only a body but a combination of body and soul—the *atma* or the self, where *atma* is the highest component of man's personality. The *atma* present in all accounts for the basic Vedantic principle of unity in diversity. We generally identify ourselves with body-mind-intellect (BMI) complex and thus live in spiritual ignorance. When we rise above the BMI idea, our outlook of life widens. This feeling manifests when we allow our individual consciousness to break the barrier of our limited ego and grow into universal consciousness. I shall quote here one definition of spirituality which is given by Sri Aurobindo, the great 20th Century philosopher of India. He said that spirituality was not high intellectuality or idealism, nor moral purity, nor austerity. It was an inner aspiration to come closer to a greater reality beyond and pervading this universe. Sri Aurobindo further says that spirituality is to feel divine, think divine and see divine. Sri Ramakrishna Paramahamsa, another great saint of India, told his disciple Swami Vivekananda that he had seen God and talked to God in the same manner as 'I see you and talk to you'. It amply proves that spirituality is not something beyond this world but can be experienced and realized while living in the world provided one has a strong ethical base. We have to become ethical first before becoming spiritual.

Spirituality can also be expressed as Yoga, truth, absolute mysticism and wisdom. In its final analysis, spirituality is a state when one obtains liberation from the cycle of birth and death. Spirituality is the science of the self. Lord Krishna states in the *Bhagavad Gita* that "Of all the science, I am the science of the self." More than 2,000 years ago, the great Greek philosopher Plato had said that the best science was the science of the self. Saint Augustine said that the goal of man was to achieve complete union with God. This is referred to as *moksha* in Indian philosophy which is the same as *nirvana* or liberation from the cycle of birth and death. This is also what Yoga aims at.

Spirituality and Religion

Can one be spiritual without being religious? Is spirituality religion specific? In the Indian context, where a vast majority of people are religious, spirituality is religion specific. In an average state of our existence, one has to raise himself to a spiritual level through his or her own religion. Most of us believe in our religion and are capable of treading the spiritual path provided we practice and live moral values as listed in our respective scriptures. Tibetan spiritual leader Dalai Lama maintains that one can be spiritual without being religious. But there are blessed souls like Shankracharya who was spiritually awakened from a very young age. Ramana Maharishi, Sri Aurobindo, Ramakrishna Paramahamsa, Swami Vivekananda, Guru Nanak, Sri Chaitanya, Lal Ded, Bhagavan Gopinathji and Sri Sri Ravi Shankar are examples of this category. But for the rest of us, it is necessary that we follow our religion in order to cultivate moral virtues and rise above the religious rituals to tread the spiritual path.

When a person understands and knows what spirituality means, he does not confine himself to his own religion but belongs to the entire mankind. His personality cannot be restricted to a particular religion, place, time or region. Spirituality is a universal concept which begins with religion but is far above and more than religion. Spiritual understanding is open to all who are self-disciplined and aware of the Divine. It is a wrong belief that spirituality is not meant for the common man. If religion turns a normal human being into a good human being, spirituality turns a good person into a righteous person. Goodness can be subjective whereas righteousness is universal.

There are differences between spirituality and religion. Religion has two sides—the personal and the social. With the personal aspect, we uplift ourselves and enter into the realm of spirituality. With its social aspect, we contribute for the betterment of the society, fully accepting that morality should subdue social order. While living in the world, we do not have to evade social responsibility. This is precisely what is meant by doing good to all creatures. Religion plays an important role in our lives even though our ultimate aim is to become spiritual. The *Mahabharata*, the great Indian epic, gives a simple meaning of religion, "Whatever holds people together is religion. We generally have a tendency to take religion as a ritual whereas it is not just a ritual but its application leading to complete transformation."

If I have to point out one basic difference between spirituality and religion, I would say that while religion can be taught or religious teachings can be imparted to a man at an average state of evolution, spirituality cannot be taught since it can only be experienced and that too when we raise our level of understanding on the foundations of morality. Religion can be misused to divide, could be exclusive and badly managed, but spirituality can never be exclusive and it would always unite. Religion can be part-time but not spirituality which is a whole-time experience.

Spiritual feeling can be equated to the fruit found on the higher branches of a tree. You can pluck the fruit from lower branches of the tree while standing on the ground but to pluck the fruit from higher branches, you have to raise yourself higher than the ground level. Similarly, to understand what spirituality means one has to raise one's level of consciousness to a plane higher than those at the level of mind and intellect.

The whole point of spirituality is to bring about a change in the living without sticking to some doctrine or dogma which is found on the surface of religion. Religion has a history whereas spirituality remains unchanged. Religion can be described whereas spirituality is beyond description, particularly at the absolute level. A spiritual experience makes us free from all forms of limitations and we see others as an extension of our own self. We understand people around us and we engage ourselves in the welfare of all with a loving attitude. Spirituality is the inner life of a man far above the rigidity of religion. A spiritual person sees the Divine pervading everything and makes no distinction between high-born or low-born and rich or poor. He feels Godhood in both pious and the wicked. A spiritual person accepts all religions of the world and bridges the gap between them with love and compassion.

Sri Aurobindo said that all would change if man could once consent to be spiritualized but his nature—mental, vital and physical—is rebellious to higher law as man loves his imperfection. Man's lower nature is the biggest obstacle on the spiritual path which has to be refined and sublimated. The more we expand and broaden our vision, the more we start visualizing what spirituality means. We have to get rid of the feeling of 'I' and 'Me' and replace it with 'We' and 'Ours' to eliminate our personal limited ego. Religious life may be the first approach to spiritual life but religion often ends in rituals, rites and ceremonies. But when one realizes that rituals and rites are only the starting point of spiritual life, he rises above them. When you are in the midst of an ocean, you cannot gauge the extent of water around you. Only when you rise higher, you get aware of the entirety of the ocean and then there is no confusion in the mind and no fear of the unknown. Similarly, when we remain within the parameters of our religion, ritual and rites, we cannot understand spirituality unless we rise above them. Those who know what spirituality is all about do not require any external assistance, belief in dogma or participation in any rituals. Spirituality blossoms in two ways. One, a spiritual person has inward love for others, and two, he develops a desire and ability to uplift others. When a person responds to joys and sorrows of others, he is in the highest state of spirituality. A religious person remains within his religion whereas a spiritual person sees all without exception in his own self and thus in the Supreme.

How can there be any lapse in righteousness of a person who knows unity of himself with others? A religious person may say that his God is exclusive, but a spiritual person knows that there is only one God who is described differently in various religions. A spiritual person knows that truth is one, sages call it by different names and it cannot be understood comprehensively by a religious person. In the life of a spiritual person, righteousness pervades every act. A spiritual person is not a part-time devotee like a religious person but he ever remains in God-consciousness. A religious person may use religion for selfish ends which is not the case of a spiritual person in whom there is no trace of selfishness. Spiritual life is not a prayer or a petition; it is a profound devoutness and silent meditation connecting to the Divine. A spiritual life does not remove us from the world but leads us deeper into it.

So how do we distinguish a spiritual person from the cluster of ordinary ones? There are certain distinctive traits of a spiritual person. He remains in a state of constant cheer, joy, bliss, love, peace and goodness. He is a sincere, honest and a well-wisher of all. He makes it a point to inspire others and give comfort to those who come in his contact. He not only understands the higher values of life but also lives them. He has equal vision, is lovable, is committed to truth, has foresight and is transparent. He utters words that are instructive. He loves everyone and feels happy to see others happy. A spiritual person is more considerate of those who are suffering. A spiritual person is like a world citizen and stays beyond caste, creed, family and lineage. A worldly person is recognized in his own area while a spiritual person is recognized all over. He develops the power of right understanding. There is no trace of selfishness in him. He is ever enthusiastic. If ever he makes a mistake, he corrects himself immediately after he has committed it. Sri Sri Ravi Shankar describes spirituality as basking in unconditional love for all, cheerfulness, beauty and enthusiasm. Spirituality gives broader understanding of life which enables a man to face conflicts and resolve them peacefully. He further says that spiritual insight makes you serve others. And when we serve others, our own problems appear smaller which can be handled easily. Politeness is the hallmark of a true spiritual person. I have come across some people who call themselves spiritual and yet display rudeness in their behaviour towards others. This is not true spirituality. A true spiritual person has time for everyone and he does not lack warmth. He is cheerful not only for himself but for others as well. In spiritual field, the way people behave is more important than what they have achieved.

India is a spiritual country, rather the spiritual capital of the world. It has produced a large number of saints, sages and seers. Among them is Sri Aurobindo, who said that India can best develop herself and serve humanity by being herself and following the law of her own nature. India being truly spiritual rejects no new light. She believes in the Vedic diction, "Let noble thoughts come to us from every side." German Indologist Max Muller confirmed this when he said that if we were to look over the whole world to find out the country most richly endowed with all the wealth, power and beauty that nature can bestow, a very paradise on earth, it is India. He further said that it is India's literature that makes our inner life perfect, comprehensive and universal. German philosopher Arthur Schopenhauer said that no study is as elevating as the study of the *Upanishads*. Appreciating Indian spiritual values and teachings of Indian sages, western historian Arnold Toynbee said that western beginning should have an Indian end if the world is not to end in self-destruction of human race. This also underscores that India is spiritual and not secular because secularism is neither spiritual nor moral.

One of the greatest saint philosophers of India, Swami Vivekananda, who put Hinduism on the world map during the parliament of religion held in Chicago in 1893, said that if there is any land on this earth which can claim to be blessed, the land where humanity has attained its highest towards gentleness, generosity, purity and calmness, it is India. India is a motherland of spirituality and if India gives up spirituality and goes after material civilization, it will be an extinct race. Dr Radhakrishnan, the well-known Indian spiritual philosopher, says that what world requires today is spiritual orientation which India can provide. From all such accounts, one can conclude that spirituality is the monopoly of India. Indian surface mind may have admitted certain western ideas but not the core, which is spiritual and shall ever remain so, expressing equality and unity of all religions and beliefs and inspired by oneness of all existence. In India, religion and spirituality do not come out from an organized belief system; people worship whatever they are related to the most.

Spirituality does not only mean living at the highest level of consciousness but also a feeling that you can strengthen the weak and enlighten the ignorant. Spirituality is a feeling that all are equal and when you are helping others, you in fact are helping yourself. In spirituality, there is no end to search and no retirement in life as you keep on learning day by day. A spiritual person's teachings pour out of the pages of experiences from the book of his life. Goal of spiritual path is self-transcendence and not self-suppression. Spiritually reformed persons are inclined to use their wisdom for general good rather than own good. A spiritually-oriented person is always kind to others in words and in deeds. Mother Teresa, the mother of afflicted humanity, said that kind words can be short and easy to speak but their echoes are truly endless. With a spiritual outlook, a man talks not of the good old days but the good now days.

Righteousness is the key to spirituality. Righteousness is rooted in morality and is projected by all religions. Truth and righteousness contain all morality—*sathyam vada dharmam chara*. Moral excellence is the foundation of spirituality. Religion can also be defined as a righteous way of living. Hinduism is called *Sanatan* or Eternal Dharma, and dharma also means righteousness. Hinduism emphasizes that ascent of man is only through the path of righteousness. In the Eightfold Noble Path of Buddhism, the keyword is Right. It talks of right view, right thought, right speech, right action, right mindfulness, right effort, right livelihood and right concentration. Buddha stressed righteousness to remove sorrow. Zoroastrianism states that there is only one path and that is the path of righteousness. The three pillars of Zoroastrianism, also referred to as the Holy Triad, consist of righteous thoughts, righteous words and righteous deeds. One of the three major duties assigned to man by Zoroastrianism is to bring a wicked person on the righteous path. Confucius, the founder of Confucianism, called righteousness a means for life-building, man-making and character-building. Confucius says that where there is righteousness in heart, there is beauty in character. According to Swami Vivekananda, character is spirituality and it is in this spirit that manliness is godliness. Righteousness and God are synonyms. Whosoever has righteousness within will brighten the world and will also find brightness in the world (*Jis ne man ka deep jalaya, usne jag ko ujala paya*). As we grow in love and virtue from inside, we shall see love and virtue from outside. If you adjust Microcosm (inside you), the Macrocosm (outside) will adjust itself for you. My own experience of spirituality tells me that we may commence from being religious but as we move ahead on the spiritual path, we transcend the rituals and fixity of religion. As a religious person, we may visit temples on specific days of the week and we may perform certain rituals regularly, but as a spiritual person, there remains no requirement to do so. For a true spiritual person, no outward worship is necessary. In any case, outward worship is only an aid to inner self-realization. A spiritual person may get the feeling of closeness to God whether inside the temple or away far from it. He remembers God at all times which is in conformity with what is said by Lord Krishna in the *Bhagavad Gita,* "Remember Me at all time and fight."

How does one define transcendence? Transcendence means moving outside the framework of one position to an entirely new one like quantum physics transcends Newtonian physics. As a religious person, one may visit temples on specific days of the week, but as a spiritual person, you do not require to do so. You get a feeling of closeness to God at all times, irrespective of whether you are inside a temple or away from it. How does one explain transcendence? I shall explain it with a small example. Transcendence means rising above or going beyond sense organs and mind surpassing phenomenal experience. Suppose you are standing on the ground in front of a multi-storey building amidst a crowd. You are being pushed around by the movement of the people on the ground floor. But as you come up on the first floor of the same building, you are not being interfered by what is happening on the ground floor. You have now transcended the ground floor experience and now you are not a victim of circumstances or environment but just an onlooker to it. You have made an effort to come to the first floor. In the same way, we have to make an effort in life to transcend pairs of opposite. You have to rise above the six pairs of opposite which are Pleasure and Pain, Gain and Loss, Victory and Defeat, Honour and Dishonour, Praise and Censure, and Heat and Cold. You also rise above Attachment and Aversion. As a rule, we can transcend only that we know and not what we do not know. For example, we can transcend goodness only when we are ourselves good. It also means that to go beyond ourselves, we must know what we are. When we understand ourselves, we understand the whole world.

Ego Hinders Spiritual Progress

To be spiritual, we must understand what is the meaning of the word Ego, which is generally understood as self-pride and which is a big hindrance on the spiritual path. Ego has two expressions. In common parlance, it means 'I am Superior,' 'I am separate from others.' Such ego hinders our interconnectedness with others. With this feeling, we cannot become spiritual because the basic concept of spirituality is that the other person is like yourself. The other meaning of ego is when you connect yourself with the body and not the soul and consider it to be the essence of man. Non-attachment with one's soul creates obstruction in self-realization. Hence, ego must be annihilated if one wants to become spiritual in the real sense.

Western psychologist Sigmund Freud describes Ego under three heads—Id, Ego and Super Ego. Id comprises the unorganized part of human personality which follows pleasure principle and seeks immediate enjoyment. It is focussed on selfishness and instant self-gratification and is responsible for basic impulses like food, water and sex. It is the dark and inaccessible part of our personality. The mind of a newborn child comes under Id as it demands immediate satisfactions. Next is Ego, which comprises the organized part of human personality and which represents reason and common sense in contrast to Id which follows passion. Ego is that part of Id which has been modified by direct influence of external world. While Id is unconscious by definition, there is conscious awareness in Ego, even though not all the operations of the Ego are conscious. Ego helps us to organize our thoughts and make sense of them and the world around us. Super Ego aims for perfection. It comprises that organized part of the personality structure which is mainly unconscious and which has individual ego ideals, spiritual goals and the psychic agency that criticizes and prohibits man's drives, fantasies, feelings and actions. The Super Ego works contradictory to the Id. The Super Ego acts in a socially oriented way whereas the Id just wants instant self-gratification. In that sense, Super Ego stands in direct opposition to Id. The Super Ego controls our sense of right, wrong and guilt. It helps us to fit into society by getting us to act in socially acceptable ways.

The word ego is taken directly from Latin where it is the nominative of first person which is translated as I or Myself. In modern day society, ego has many meanings like inflated self-worth, sense of pride, sense of separateness or even selfishness. In Indian spiritual language, ego is identification of oneself with BMI complex and not the *atma*, the real man. Its Sanskrit equivalent is *ahamkara*. In an average state of our existence, the idea that I am the body is very strong which makes us live in body consciousness and not universal consciousness of our soul. Such an identification makes us think and act in a non-divine way. We accept that we are the doer and enjoyer of our actions and at the same time getting a feel of happiness and sorrow as they come. When we take credit of our actions we feel we are superior to others and a feeling of separateness enters into us. This sense of separateness is maximum at physical level and starts decreasing when we raise our level of consciousness to mental and intellectual levels. It becomes Zero only at spiritual level when we consider ourselves as pure consciousness which is the actual doer of actions. Then there is no I and Me which is a part of our lower nature, separating us from God.

To think you are great while others are not is egotism. Actions performed under the impulse of ego are those actions which are performed for image building and not for world solidarity or for good of others. Saint Ramakrishna divides ego into two parts calling them higher ego or ripe ego and lower ego or unripe ego. Ripe ego is self-esteem while unripe ego is pride. There is a story in the *Mahabharata* which mentions Ashtavakra and Janaka. Ashtavakra, the teacher of king seer Janaka, compares ego with a black serpent with a poisonous bite. 'I am the doer' is the essence of ego which involves us with sensual objects and in the process pollutes our mind with sensuality, bringing about spiritual annihilation. Thus we see, as long as ego remains, there can be no spiritual progress.

How to Overcome Ego?

Sri Ramakrishna gave a solid solution to overcome ego which is his *Mahamantra*. He said let the rascal ego be the servant of God. The rope that is tied and knotted will lose its ability to bind if it is burnt. What looks like a rope and the knot is only the appearance because it is burnt into ashes. A servant does not work for himself but works for his master. The servant is free and not affected by profit or loss but the master is. Ego is totally annihilated by surrendering to God. The way out of ego is to maintain I am not the doer, I am pure consciousness, I am *Brahman*.

There is a proverbial saying, 'As one thinks, so one becomes'. Work really becomes worship when done by effacing one's ego and resigning to God. When knowledge about true-self dawns, the ego disappears. Ego also represents negative traits such as anger, greed and hate. If we get rid of the negativity within and fill us with positive ideas, the ego loses its bite. And allowing negative ideas to stay within strengthens the ego.

Relationship between spirituality and ego is given by spiritual saint Paramhamsa Yogananda who defined spirituality as ever diminishing identification with the little self or ego. Dr Radhakrishnan said that when ego is lost, its false identification with body disappears and it is illumined by the Self. Sri Sri Ravi Shankar says that I or ego, though a tiny atom, becomes miserable when identified with body. When associated with spirit, it becomes divine. Ego causes discomfort and does not let love flow. Ego desires to prove and possess. When there is nothing to prove and nothing to possess, ego dissolves. Total dedication leaves no room for ego. Both western psychologists and Indian saints agree in general that ego in the final analysis should be divinized. An egoist person can be easily recognized by his body language even if you do not talk to him. His face is serious and eyes unromantic and he does not stop to listen to you. He has a self-seeking attitude and is seldom negotiable.

Spirituality is our cultural heritage. Culture can be defined in many ways—ethical values, spiritual values, identity thoughts and behavioural pattern. Culture is a complex whole that includes knowledge, beliefs, morals, laws and customs. In Hinduism, there is no difference between religion and culture. India is one of the few civilizations which has a chequered history and unbroken continuity of culture and civilization. To focus on spirituality is India's uniqueness. TS Eliot called religion the base of culture. As far as India is concerned, it has a sophisticated cultural heritage. The aim of Indian culture is to achieve not temporary but permanent happiness. Indian culture is not otherworldly as some western writers may feel. Foundation of Indian culture is built on three noble acts which are sacrifice (*yajna*), austerity (*tapa*) and charity (*dana*). These are beautifully explained in the *Bhagavad Gita* which says that only those who practise these virtues can lead a good life manifesting their true personality. The main features of Indian culture are tolerance, sense of synthesis and universal outlook. Tolerance means acceptance of others and their ideas. It means accommodating others, accepting others, giving space to others and living in unconditional acceptance in a spirit of love and forgiveness.

The two terms which are much interconnected and often not well understood are culture and civilization. Culture is one word which describes the quality of citizenship in a country. Civilization comprises all technologies and material instruments devised by man in his endeavour to control condition of life. Survival of Indian civilization is primarily due to its predominant spiritual character where a person is pure and inwardly polished and places himself lovingly at the disposal of the needy. He is said to be truly cultured. We call a person more cultured when he controls his impulses and instincts. A civilized person, though impressive outwardly, may not be cultured. But a cultured person is also a civilized person. We can say that a civilized person is impressive outwardly whereas a cultured man is impressive inwardly. Western sociologist MacIver said that civilization is what we have and culture is what we are. You can take away from me what I have but you cannot take away from me what I am.

Culture thus stands taller than civilization. Civilization is the body and culture is the mind. Sri Sathya Sai Baba, another great spiritual leader of India, describes culture as giving up bad thoughts and bad actions and cultivating sacred thoughts and noble ideas. Culture resides in any nation's consciousness of life, reflected in its thoughts, ideals and aspirations. Culture is not just art or literature, or dancing or music as it is understood by an average mind. Culture is a pattern of behaviour generally accepted by people. A man of culture imposes restraints on himself but there is a joy and pride in acceptance of such restraints. Wider meaning of culture is self-control. Culture is expressed through languages, art, philosophy, religion, education, social habits and customs. Various forms of media including radio, TV and newspapers are also parts of culture. When we talk about cultural heritage, it includes all aspects of human values transmitted to us by our ancestors from generation to generation.

The UNESCO's definition of culture is total accumulation of material objects, ideas, symbols, beliefs, sentimental values and social forms which are passed on from one generation to another. Culture as a complex whole includes knowledge, beliefs, moral laws and customs. It is the way of life of people living together at one place. Transcendentalism is the characteristic feature of Indian culture but at the base, Indian culture is robust positivism which has zest for life, and is expressive in art, literature, music and dance.

Sri Aurobindo says that the whole root of difference between Indian and European culture springs from the spiritual aim of

Indian civilization. Spirituality is the cornerstone on which is built the edifice of Indian life and culture. The strength of Indian culture lies in scriptures such as the *Bhagavad Gita,* the *Upanishads,* the *Ramayana,* the *Mahabharata* and various saints who have appeared on our soil from time to time and have taught the masses through their actions and words. Life cannot be lived solely by mere externalities because man has the power of exceeding himself. Dr Radhakrishnan said that man is a duality. He is capable of doing great things under spiritual influence and is also capable of doing very low things when disassociated from spirituality. Indian culture is rooted in spiritualism and the *summum bonum* of Indian culture is truth, non-violence, love, peace and righteousness.

A cultured man is respected wherever he goes. His words carry weight. What we call Indology is the study of Indian culture from an essentially Indian point of view. Indian culture has a firm belief in the Vedic concept of *vasudhaiva kutumbakam* which means that the whole world is one household or family that aims at establishment of peace, friendship and brotherhood in the world.

What is happiness for me is happiness for others. What is painful for me is painful for others. Indian culture is a composite culture. India is a land which has witnessed invasions and dominations from outside where many tribes have come and gone, leaving an imprint on the indigenous culture. The composite Indian culture has accommodated the best of other cultures true to the spirit of the Vedic belief that the world is one family. India learns and absorbs from other cultures yet remaining anchored on its own value system that forms the rich Indian culture. India believes in Vedic dictum that allows noble thoughts to come to us from all directions and sources. India is, therefore, often described as a cultural superpower right from the time of its birth.

How does a spiritual person act? Life which is spiritual has its impact and influence on every aspect of existence including the works which one undertakes. A spiritual person has oneness of thought, words and deeds. In his actions, he follows the dictum of spirituality. A spiritual person follows skill in action and is not concerned with spiritual matters but is equally concerned with the development of the humanity and the world. He follows love in action. Love in action means 'I do things for others with Love as I do for myself.'

Spirituality in action means solving the problems of others based on the fact that all are equal and when I am helping others, I am in fact helping myself. To him, the whole world is his own, but he has no sense of possession. This is in tune with what king Janaka said in the *Ashtavakra Gita,* "In one way, nothing belongs to me; in another way, everything is mine." This would also mean that if you possess things, there is no harm but it would be a tragedy if things possess you. Therefore, make the world your own without allowing the world to possess you. You should belong to the world but the world does not belong to you.

Indira Gandhi, one of India's prime ministers, once remarked that India is rich in its philosophy and culture but she was not able to project this to people because so many of Indians look at it superficially. This is very true because most Indians do not know India's greatness and the values it stands for. The world knows more about India than Indians do. This must be reversed.

There are no short cuts in learning and assimilating higher values of life. Short cuts often lead to wrong routes. To understand noble ideas, one must walk every inch of ground. The nobility which one acquires must be put into practice and this must be exhibited through one's own conduct, otherwise its learning is of little or no use. What is the use of dark dense clouds which do not rain and do not benefit earth and plants? Similarly, knowledge in mind if not translated in conduct is hardly of any use.

There is a general tendency that when we lean towards religion and spirituality, we disregard science. That should not be so. We should not value science over religion or religion over science. There should be a harmonized fusion of science and religion. Both science and religion are based on knowledge and reason. Difference is only in their application.

Religion explores metaphysical truths whereas science gives truth about the physical world. In science, we learn to do; in religion, we learn to be. Of science and religion, religion has an edge over science. Science cannot explain the laws of human life—why someone is born in misery and others in joy. Religion can explain this on the basis of the law of karma and the theory of reincarnation. Science is not a substitute for virtue. It cannot make societies more and more sensible. Religion is capable since it is the source of all virtues.

Science and technology cannot replace age-old spiritual values which have been largely responsible for the progress of world civilization. Science cannot teach love, sympathy and humility. It is religion that teaches these besides all that is good. Of science and spirituality science should not be discredited. Science prepares us for higher wisdom. Even though wisdom is different from scientific knowledge, it is not separate from it. Scientific knowledge prepares for higher wisdom as it dispels the darkness of mind. But of the two, spirit is higher than matter. Even Napoleaon acknowledged this when he said that the spirit will conquer the sword. Science is a work of the last 350–400 years whereas history of religion dates back as far as the *Vedas*. Shankracharya had said that spiritual ideas are best spread when they are understood and practised by people of more than ordinary good qualities. This obviously means that spirituality is higher than goodness.

Does one have to leave his home and go to forests for spiritual elevation? Buddha was asked the same question by his wife when Buddha visited his home after achieving enlightenment. Buddha said that it was not necessary to leave one's home and go to a secluded place for spiritual awakening. Spiritual awakening can be obtained while being a member of the household. This is in conformity with the views in the *Bhagavad Gita*. It says that for attaining spiritual wisdom one should live in the world and not renounce it. Leaving society and going to a jungle or a mountain is a lower form of spirituality. But one should not be affected by the events of the world while staying in it. One should live like a lotus flower which grows and stays in water but is not affected by the water all around it. To be spiritual one has to be peaceful under disturbed environment. Also there is no opposition between spiritual advancement and material advancement. If you are advancing spiritually, it does not block your material advancement.

To be spiritual means we should be morally sound having transcended our religion. To be morally upright we must become a good human being. To be genuinely good we must be simple as simplicity is a sign of perfection. And when we are simple with a good disposition we acquire the ability to change ourselves and to uplift ourselves on to a spiritual plane. We shall now study these three qualities under separate heads for our deeper understanding. When a man is controlled by spirit he is a man of steady wisdom, when he is controlled by mind he is an ordinary man and when he is controlled by senses, he is no different than an animal.

Be a Good Human Being

Before we attempt to become anything else, we must try to become good human beings. Goodness has a far fetched implication since in that it leads to harmony in the world. When we are anchored on goodness, we shall ever feel contended, happy and peaceful in whatsoever situations we may find ourselves in. Goodness is the only investment that never fails. Even God is deeply concerned about good people. God says in the *Bhagavad Gita* that for the protection of the good, He incarnates in the world from time to time. Today, India lacks good human beings. We realize this when we read daily newspapers which carry tales of immoral deeds of our countrymen. What is disturbing is that such things are happening in a country where morality took firm roots before moving out to the other parts of the world. We are inclined to believe that people who are educated and are occupying high positions in the society are good people. This is not so because goodness is above formal education and intellectuality. Literacy is a means of becoming good but is not goodness itself. An educated person is a civilized person whereas a good person is a cultured man. A civilized person is impressive outwardly whereas a cultured man is impressive inwardly.

If you are good and do good to others, you are on your way to Godliness. Being good is being morally sound; being good is being virtuous; being good is acting righteously and having a good behaviour and good character; being good is to have goodwill for all, and most importantly, being good means good thoughts. To practise goodness in our day-to-day life is a great austerity and a great discipline. Goodness is within the reach of everyone, provided one has the conviction. Goodness fills our heart with compassion and unconditional love and we become a source of positive thoughts. Not only we enrich our life with good thoughts but we also give comfort to those who come in our contact. By doing good to others and by being good ourselves, we move on the path of God as it is the best way of God worship. Goodness is the foundation of righteousness and spirituality. We have to develop goodness first and then express it in society.

To be good means to think good, to speak good, to hear good and to see good. To think good, we have to develop a thinking mind rather than a pleasure-seeking mind. A thinking mind shall radiate good thoughts and good thoughts shall produce good speech and good action. Doing comes from thinking. That is why Swami Vivekananda said that we should fill up our mind with the highest ideals and high thoughts and out of that will come great work. To hear good means not to hear ill of others and avoid listening to irrelevant talks. Hearing good also means to seek company of holy people who give noble ideas through their conversation. To see good would mean to avoid seeing anything obscene. There can be no real goodness in man without self-examination, self-investigation, self-introspection and self-consciousness. When you become conscious of your weaknesses, there arises an urge to rise above them.

Great teachers of the world have emphasized goodness in different ways. Swami Vivekananda said that to be good and to do good is the whole of religion. Greek philosopher Plato said that good people do not need laws to tell them to act responsibly. Buddha said that good deeds are eternal. He placed goodness on the highest pedestal in his teachings. He summed up his entire philosophy by saying 'Be Good and Do Good'. Buddha equated goodness with righteousness. He said that one can overpower sufferings of life by righteousness. In his right-fold path of Fourth Noble Truth, Buddha said that sufferings can be removed by adopting right attitude towards what all you do in life. Buddha further said that good deeds are eternal. Neither fire nor wind, birth or death can erase good deeds. In the *Bhagavad Gita*, Lord Krishna said that for the doer of good, there is no destruction here in the world and hereafter. He further said that the doer of good never comes by evil. Islam says that God only accepts that which is good. God blesses those who are good and are engaged in good work. *The Bible* says that doing good in the present assures the kingdom of heaven of tomorrow as we are heir to our deeds. Goodness cleanses our mind and soul of the evil accumulated therein of the past births. Goodness fills our heart with compassion and selfless love which enables us to look beyond the limits of our mind.

A good person is a good finder as well. A good person sees goodness in others and also helps others to see good in themselves. He projects good side in any situation. He encourages a man by showing his good side. A good person talks to people in such a way that everyone feels that the talk was addressed to him. He values what others say. He listens and accommodates others' views without imposing his own. A good person has developed an eye to observe good alone. His mind does not focus on the bad side of a person. This is the real test of a good person. If you are good internally, your eyes will only catch what is good externally from a mixture of good and bad. That is why it is said that good people are a blessing for mankind.

A good person is ever prepared for the welfare of all. He is not indifferent to wrongs done to others in front of his eyes. We all have the strength of goodness in us in some proportion. What is needed is to manifest it with right thinking. There is one bit advantage of being good—you stand firm on your ground whether you are applauded or blamed. When you believe you are good, you do not need any public support for your good actions. A good person is indifferent to criticism against himself. When one is looking good outwardly, one is not certain how long he would feel good inwardly. On the contrary, when one is good inwardly, he will always feel good and look good outwardly. As a person improves his goodness inwardly, his looking good outwardly increases in the same proportion.

One should look for good in every situation and one will almost always find it. There is no difficulty in becoming a good human being, provided one is prepared to discriminate between what is good and what is not and stick to what is good. Highlighting the value of good people, Swami Vivekananda said that a system may be good but if the system is not manned by good people, it fails.

To be good is not the ultimate goal of our life. In the final analysis, we have to transcend goodness and get ourselves firmly established in Truth. Good actions promote spirituality but they do not liberate us from the bondage. It is only the knowledge of ultimate Truth that liberates us from bondage and gives us the much-desired total freedom. This is what Lord Krishna explained to Arjuna in the *Bhagavad Gita* and also gave him the means of doing so. Purity of mind is the means which is to be attained through the practice of Yoga and acquiring divine attributes. A good act does not need any reward. It is a reward by itself. A good person makes others feel good with his presence and conversation. Psychologist William James said that being good means to lead a good life based on good habits developed through constant practices of virtues. Even if we are successful in our worldly life, we should always try to be good inwards. Then only can we solve our problems, as all problems are inside and all solutions of life are also inside a man. A good person possesses sun-like affection, river-like generosity and earth-like hospitality.

Swami Vivekananda said that the basis of all systems, social and political rests on goodness. A nation is good because men are good. Nothing in this world is without significance, not a particle is meaningless. None is bad, all are relatively good. What people call bad is less good in the same manner as falsity is less true. Chinese philosopher Confucius said that a good person is one who loves all and speaks good of all. Lao Tze, the founder of Taoism, said that goodness is a virtue. Cultivate this virtue in yourself, in family, in village and in universe. One should not be selective in his behaviour towards others. One should be good to people who are good to you and also good to people not good to you.

Simplicity is a Sign of Perfection

The well-known maxim 'simple living and high thinking' is very true. Unless we are simple, we cannot think high. High thinking is nothing but unselfish thinking. We generally think about our own self and about our gains, but we seldom think about others, their problems and possible solutions. We behave with others as per their status in life. In this way, we acquire a split personality. We can overcome this trend by adopting simplicity in life.

There is no greatness where there is no simplicity. Simplicity is the characteristic of greatness. How does one define simplicity? Simplicity is perfect alignment of one's thoughts, words and deeds. Greatest truths are simple but we make them difficult. When you are simple, your outer and inner life coincides. It is because when one is simple, there are no traces of crookedness in him. We make ourselves complicated by splitting our personality. Inwardly we are something but outwardly we are different. Outwardly we are different in our conduct because somehow we mistakenly feel that our outward pattern of behaviour should be different under different circumstances. We present ourselves as what we are really not. Such a person may or may not fool others but surely he is fooling himself by making his life difficult since he is not adhering to his natural behaviour.

A modern man does not like himself to be branded as a simpleton. He equates simplicity with unimpressiveness, backwardness and even stupidity. He feels that a simple person cannot be successful in life. Such feelings are the product of narrow-mindedness. We have seen that simple persons have done great things in life. They are not only successful but also perfect in all aspects of life.

Simplicity leads to truthfulness. A simple person sees things as they are and presents them without adding or subtracting anything out of them. In such cases, where is the scope to tell a lie? Simple persons have a clear conscience free from any ambiguity. They create plenty of space in their mind to allow noble thoughts to come to them. The space is created by virtue of expelled contradictions and falsities from within which are found aplenty in materialistic people. Simple people earn all comforts of life through fair means. Truly simple persons are at ease with themselves and with others.

Simplicity is not well understood by a worldly man since he is attached to presentation of truth in a complicated way. A worldly man will present things to others with distorted facts as he feels that making lengthy statements out of a small thing is the only way to impress others. He is used to making mountains out of moles. And if you present things in a complicated manner, it covers up your lack of knowledge of the subject. It is also a fact that to explain something in a simple way is not that easy. It requires thorough understanding of the subject. It requires talent. The more knowledge a person has of a subject, the more he would be inclined to put across his views in a simple way. And when something is presented in a simple manner, it will be received well and would be well understood. The same goes for simple writing. There are writers who show off their knowledge in their writings, even if it is not appreciated by common readers. A good writing is one which can be grasped by everyone.

Simplicity means doing what is necessary and which makes sense. It means keeping a balance in life. It also means keeping life as an open book. Simple living means living with what is necessary for living. It also means living in moderation without over-possession. When a person is simple, the thought process is so evolved that it corresponds to simple living and high thinking. Simplicity comes by living a regulated and organized life. Simplicity can be applied in all spheres of life—dress, food, talk, behaviour and in our interaction with others. For being simple, one has to be oneself. The words of a simple person are dynamic and such words pierce into others. A simple person leads a stress free life since he is pure and truthful at the core of his being. Sri Aurobindo said that to express harmony in all things simplicity is the best.

Simplicity is a prerequisite for spiritual advancement. As long as one does not become simple as a child, one does not get divine illumination. Unless the man is simple, he cannot recognize God, the simplest and the purest one. All our spiritual saints who achieved greatness in spiritual field were simple in true sense of their being. If you read the lives of Sri Ramakrishna, Swami Vivekananda, Sri Aurobindo, Maharishi Ramana and Mahatma Gandhi, one thing was common in all of them—they were simple and led a very simple life. Whatever they wanted to convey was free from any kind of multiplicity. They all were men of character with deep concern for the welfare and well being of others. Among them, Mahatma Gandhi was not only a simple person but simplicity personified. He led a flower-like simple, pure life. With his simplicity, he identified himself with the masses of India. He is the best example to demonstrate how a simple man generates high thinking.

Lao Tzu said that simplicity is the key to success. He defined simplicity as the foundation of culture and inner life. According to him, simplicity is superior to living a simple life. A man has to be simple inwards whatever his mode of living be. A thing is called superior not because it is difficult. Simplicity consists in things being simple and easy and at the same time being effective for most rather than a few. It is one thing to understand simplicity yourself. It is another thing to get the same things understood by others. It is here that simplicity plays a very important role—the way you express yourself to others in simple understandable words. Only a simple person can do so. When we are simple and ordinary, there are better chances for us to become extraordinary.

Change to Uplift Yourself

One of the essentials for uplifting ourselves is to possess a conviction that we can become a better human being. When we try to change others, we fail miserably, but when we change ourselves, we inspire others. Yudhistira says in the *Mahabharata* that it is not that people do not know their weaknesses; it is just that they do not put in enough efforts to change themselves.

There is a need to change ourselves from being not so good to good and from good to better and so on. These require special efforts on our part. Changing ourselves from being not so good to bad and from bad to worse requires no effort at all. This change takes place automatically when one allows himself to be dictated by his outgoing mind and senses without exercising self-control. The biggest obstacle in the process of self-evolution is to firmly hold the view that a man cannot change the nature he is born with. This view is totally unfounded. There is nothing more harmful than to hold this belief as it closes all doors of self-improvement. In broader sense, changing yourself means having the courage to face worldly life correctly. Sri Aurobindo warned that if one does not have the courage to face worldly life, he will perpetually remain in misery and suffering and will never be able to go through inner struggle of changing his own nature for self-elevation.

An ordinary man is a slave to his inborn tendencies and inclinations which we call our nature, and which are generally directed toward the outer world through outgoing senses. This prohibits a man to raise his mental level to acquire a higher state of consciousness. Such a person does not hesitate to criticize others on their behaviour without realizing that he himself possesses the same behavioural pattern and is equally prone to criticism by others. All of us want the world to become good, but, at the same time, we do not make any worthwhile effort to contribute from our side to make the world a nice place to live. The world, a nation or a society comprises people and only when people living therein become good by changing themselves the world can become good. Mahatma Gandhi had once said that we must be the change we wish to see in the world. This statement highlights that each one of us must first of all remove the faults from within instead of observing faults of others. For that, a man must accept that he can change himself with self-effort.

As per the karma theory, a man is born with certain traits which we call our nature. The path of least resistance is to allow the nature to take control of us and we become a witness to the play of nature. It lies in our hands to break away from the control of our nature and make our life purposeful both at materialistic and spiritual level. If we are born in a poor family, we can become rich; if we are physically weak, we can become strong. Similarly, if a man is born with wicked tendencies, he can turn noble, and if he is ignorant, he can become wise. Dr Radhakrishnan said that a man's nature does not absolutely determine his actions. Our past karmas may determine our ancestry and heredity but we have the freedom of choice in the present life to evolve ourselves to a higher state of existence or move downward to a lower one.

Dr Radhakrishnan equated life to a game of bridge where the cards are dealt. The cards may be good or bad. We can play the game well or play it badly. A skilful player may have a poor hand and yet win the game while a bad player with a good hand loses it. If a man plays the game of life skillfully, applying his power of determination and intelligent will, then he would give his approval to only those acts which are righteous. He would not act blindly as per his impulses and passions. When he does so, the grip of his inborn nature on him slackens. The *Bhagavad Gita* said that Yoga is skill in action.

In our average state of awareness, we live a stereotype programmed life. This makes us monotonous and uncreative and we refuse to grow inwardly. In the words of Sri Aurobindo, it is only by constant inner growth that we obtain unfailing interest in life. If our aim is to grow inwardly, then we must assume responsibility to control and resolve conflicts within which hinder our self-evolution. We must accept responsibility for our deeds. When we do that, we do not invest our time on doing things that drag us downwards. Each day in our life should be considered a new day and we should step into new day without any baggage or preconceived notions which usually become obstacles in our growth. Our ultimate aim of life should be to move to the highest state of consciousness to realize divinity within us.

To bring about a qualitative change in us, we have to evaluate our weaknesses and strengths through self-analysis or self-introspection. After identifying our weaknesses, we have to take the necessry steps to eliminate them with our good qualities which all of us have in some proportion. The biggest evil in man is selfishness which restricts everyone exclusively to our materialistic gains. Unless selfishness is removed, we can neither be of any use to others nor can we change ourselves. One quality which is found in all great men of the world is that they were all selfless workers.

Russian novelist and thinker Leo Tolstoy said that everyone thinks of changing the world but no one thinks of changing himself. To change ourselves, we must accept our responsibility of what we are and what we want to be. We have to make ourselves responsible for ourselves. Responsibility makes you work at your best. We must rectify, reform and correct ourselves so that we acquire confidence and determination for changing others. If you want to change the world for the better, just try to better yourself. Subjective world rules the objective; change the subject, the object will change. The more we grow in love, virtue and holiness, the more love, virtue and holiness we shall see outside. Reforming oneself is the gateway to reform humanity.

It is said that nothing in the world requires our attention except uplifting ourselves. Do yourself what you like others to do such as practising truth and honesty or helping those in distress. Also avoid doing what you despise in others. Do not exclude yourself while talking of the weaknesses of the society as you yourself are not beyond reproach and are a part of that society. Acquire courage and confidence to declare that you can become a better person by changing yourself. Even fate surrenders before men with such determination. Such persons when faced with difficulties are convinced that they have the will and the capacity to overcome the difficulties. They know that God helps only those who help themselves. Changing oneself for the better may appear a difficult task but it can be accomplished slowly and steadily. Rome was not built in a day but it was built nonetheless. Whatever we wish ourselves to be, we have the power to make ourselves.

> *There are only two ways to live your life. One is as though nothing is a miracle. The other is as though everything is a miracle.*
>
> **Albert Einstein**

Personality Development

Mind is the creator of everything. You should therefore guide it to create only good.

Paramahamsa Yogananda

To develop our personality, we must know what it constitutes of. As per the Indian thought, a man has two distinct entities—soul and matter. The essence of a man is soul or *atma* which comprises 90 per cent of a living being. The matter in us consists of body, mind and intellect. While the soul is constant, unchangeable, indestructible; body, mind and intellect within a man are variable and can be uplifted to a higher level of existence. Though the soul inside a being is limitless, as a man is essentially divine, it is egotism, narrow vision and a lack of commitment towards social growth that make us self-centred.

Personality development is not only laterally expansive, it is more importantly a vertical growth. When we define total health, it does not mean absence of disease but the health of all constituents of the body—physical, mental, intellectual and spiritual. A healthy person is one who is morally sound, has his body in good shape and has a healthy mind and intellect. He is the one who can differentiate between matter and spirit, between right and wrong, and between good and bad. The body is the temple wherein God resides in the form of our soul. It is our duty to keep the body clean and healthy. Ill health of body can affect the growth of mind and intellect.

Body and mind are interrelated. If the mind remains healthy, the body will remain healthy as body follows the mind. Mind's influence on body is deeper than the influence of body on mind. Strong mind faces difficulty squarely and does not run away from it. Such a mind does not succumb to worldly temptations. In the process of personality development, the body needs to be looked after and its health should not be ignored. However, it is the development of the mind and intellect which would ultimately assist us to become spiritual. Our senses stimulate the mind and if mind is not kept under the control of intellect, a person is liable to act impulsively. To control the mind, intellect has to play the role of a mentor to keep its activities under check. Interconnectedness between body, mind, intellect and soul is beautifully explained in the *Bhagavad Gita* where Lord Krishna said that senses (body) are great but superior to senses is mind, superior to mind is intellect and superior to intellect is *atma* inside.

Intellect or *buddhi* performs three functions of discrimination, judgment and decision. Superior most constituent of man's personality is soul which is unimaginable, eternal, inconceivable, unamendable and indestructible. It is all powerful being, a spark of Supreme *Brahman* or God Almighty. Therefore, personality development would imply raising our level of consciousness to its highest level.

To become spiritual, a man must have a sound moral base which enables him to transcend mental and intellectual levels of his personality. All human beings are potentially divine. Since the soul is a ray of supreme, our core consciousness is absolutely pure. This purity within is required to be manifested outwardly to regulate our conduct as per the pure inner consciousness. Though our inner consciousness is pure, it does not reveal its pure state in our conduct because it is filtered through our BMI complex. Due to this, our outward conduct is dictated by the quality of our mind. For example, water will seem coloured if poured into a colourful bottle. If the colour of the bottle is green, the water will look the same shade, even though it is colourless. When a ray of light is reflected through a mirror covered with dust, the reflected light would lose its original state and look distorted as the reflecting material is not clean. Similarly, the soul inside all living beings is divine or absolute pure consciousness, but the outward conduct is different from man to man depending upon the quality of man's BMI complex which, in this case, becomes the reflecting material through which the divine ray is reflected or filtered. The divine ray is filtered through our mind carrying our inborn nature which obstructs divinity to manifest outwardly in totality. For those who are spiritually evolved, there is no contradiction between their inner consciousness and outer conduct. But majority of human beings have an ordinary level of consciousness and therefore their outer conduct is coloured by the state of their mind. Spiritually evolved persons have a pure and clean mind which allows the divine ray to pass through it without any obstruction. They are the same from inside and outside.

Our actions originate from our mind and are guided by our thought process. As one thinks, so he acts and so he becomes. Our actions are our frozen thoughts. A thought is like a force which is fuelled by attention. Unless our mind and intellect are pure, our actions may not be righteous all the times. For matching our outer behaviour with our inner being, we have to attain purity of mind by practising moral virtues as given in our scriptures. We have to cleanse our mind of all the impurities it has gathered through our actions, thoughts and words of this life and also of past lives which we have lived. The term personality development aims at raising our level of existence to the highest spiritual level so that we follow a righteous behaviour and pattern. We may differ in our interests, careers, behavioural relationship or way of living, but we all have the same *atma*, a fraction of the divine. There is spiritual unity even though there are differences at the physical, mental and intellectual level of our personality. Since we all are spiritual at the core, we can reach the highest level of our personality.

We may examine different levels of our personality to see how best we can live at that level for our progress. Living at the physical level of our personality means that we are living at the level of sense pleasures. Since our senses are outgoing, it is very natural that we get attracted to the sense objects. At the physical level, we also look for body comforts. We want a shelter for us and also food and clothes. We also look for a reasonably good job to earn money to sustain our worldly living. There is no harm in looking for means to satisfy such needs as long we do not develop greed for them. As far as our senses are concerned, we have to control them and not reject them. Sense objects may be enjoyed keeping the purity of mind in view but we should not get attached to them. Eyes will see what is attractive, ears will hear sweet melodies but we should not give them complete freedom to see or hear as they like. We should know how to exercise control over them. Beauty must be seen and appreciated in whatever form it is presented because beauty is God's handwriting. Never miss any opportunity to see anything beautiful. Anyone who retains the ability to see beauty never misses on the joy of life.

Mind is a very important aspect of human personality. It is a forerunner of our good state of existence. If mind is pure, happiness follows like one's shadow that never leaves. Mind has a tendency to remain in the past or future but seldom in the present. It also likes to get attached to people. It is an instrument of cognition. Mind is the most important factor in the development of human personality. Different states of mind could be described as the states of depression, excitement and restlessness. It is an essential part of our personality. Mind overall has four faculties—the Mind Stuff (*chitta*), the Mind (*manas*), the Intellect (*buddhi*) and the Ego (*ahamkara*). The Mind is usually dominated by likes and dislikes which disturb its peace. The objective world as such does not create any problem on our mind. Problems are created by a mind dominated by likes and dislikes. The Mind is described by our sages as a river with two opposite courses: one moving towards good and the other towards evil. The good one moves in the channel of discrimination and leads to liberation. The evil one moves in the non-discriminatory field and leads to bondage. What strengthens mind is self-awareness, concentration, positivism, optimism, willpower and knowledge. What weakens mind is fear, insecurity, clouded thinking, self-centeredness and ignorance.

Mind is ever restless, dwelling on the past and future but seldom on the present. A restless mind is compared with a monkey who is intoxicated and bitten by a scorpion. Mind generates thoughts and if they are not controlled, they can bring down the man to its lowest level. Mastering the mind is mastering life. The best way to control mind is not to get identified with irrelevant thoughts. To control mind, we must learn to discard those thoughts which are not beneficial. The art of living lies not only in what we choose but also what we discard. Thoughts are like fire fuelled by attention. By not paying attention to thoughts, we leave the mind unattended. Wrestling with thoughts tantamount to giving attention to thoughts. It is very pertinent to state here what the *Bhagavad Gita* talks about mind control. It says that a controlled mind is our greatest friend and an uncontrolled mind our worst enemy.

To control mind, we should learn to be silent as keeping a silent mind is as good as God's worship. The *Bhagavad Gita* gives a beautiful study of mind. With a careful study of mind, one can detect the most powerful tendencies of mind that arise. Then we can know why mind behaves in a particular way. Once this is known, we can take corrective measures to put the mind on to the righteous path.

At the mental level, we are confronted with human emotions. Emotions are to do with our feelings. They enable us to experience different facets of life. A man is born with emotions. He cannot live without them. But we have to guide emotions between emotional and psychological life. Emotions are like flood water, which, if not checked, will overflow. Therefore, emotionally we should be healthy. Emotionally evolved persons are more balanced in relationship with others as they have no negative emotions. They are more successful than a man of extraordinary intelligencc. Man should be emotionally soft to remain mentally calm.

Mind is also referred to as the sixth sense because if it is not kept under control, it shall follow the senses. We should also keep in check negative emotions like hatred, anger, greed and jealousy and replace them with positive emotions like love, compassion and equal vision. We must learn to empathize with others and develop a sense of oneness with all. This is the beginning of spiritual life.

Another very important aspect of mental development is that we should give life to our relationship with others by being actively involved in it. A passive and negative approach towards our relationship will not permit our relationship to grow. But relationship need not get too personal. We can have relationship with anyone without being attached to the person concerned, provided we have a pure mind. A sage gets attached to all his disciples without belonging to anyone. We should never look for a comfort zone in our relationship. Problems activate mind that helps in development of one's personality. That is why it is said that challenges are a way to progress.

Mental development is also referred to as development of heart; not the physical heart but the conceptual centre of mind which radiates positive emotions like love, compassion, equal vision, etc. The positive emotions act like grease to our intellectual strength. It is through our heart and feelings that we gain goodwill of others. It is our heart which tells us that compassion, love and gratitude are bigger than anger, hatred and jealousy. And it also tells us that detachment is bigger than attachment. Lao Tzu said that he who controls others may be powerful but he who has mastered himself is mightier.

At intellectual level, we rely on reason and power of discrimination to decide how we should live our life. Intellect is also the seat of enthusiasm. German philosopher Immanuel Kant laid utmost emphasis on reason when he said that enlightenment is maturity through the use of reason. Reason kills un-reason just as science kills un-science. A well-developed intellect is an agent of self-suggestion, self-advice and self-persuasion. The intelligence which the *atma*-inclined intellect generates is spiritual intelligence. This is also called *buddhi yoga*. It gives the power of intuition which is intelligent anticipation. Intuition is something which drives you forward and helps you to see situations before making decisions. Intuition is a creative feeling of knowing beyond logic and ever wants to help you. It is also referred to as new capacity of understanding, new vision of things and their understanding beyond sense power and rationality dominated by divine presence. A true intuition can only come to the mind which is pure and free from desires and passions, where inner life is fully integrated in the practice of self-control and mental discipline. Being creative is to see same things as everybody else but thinking of something new and different.

Creativity

Creativity is the ability to come up with new ideas and solve problems in original way. A creative person is problem-less. He is friendly and never blames others. He is enthusiastic, flexible and an optimist. He does not tread the beaten track. Intuitive message generally comes from subconscious mind. At intellectual level, we can differentiate between right and wrong, good and bad, virtue and vice and develop the courage to do what we want to do. Intellect gives us the power of distinguishing between the two opposite choices. There is a Sanskrit saying that a man who is devoid of the power of distinguishing what is good from what is harmful is no better than a cow except that he eats rice and not grass. Actions performed under the guidance of intellect are always good actions. A well-developed intellect transmits powerful thoughts which have an effect on others. One thing must be clearly understood that intellectuality by itself is not wisdom. An intellectual could be more concerned about himself whereas a wise person is more concerned about others. Greek philosopher Pythagoras said that wisdom is the power which moves man to change himself. Socrates said that power and wealth should be subordinate to the quest of wisdom. One equation between intellectuality and wisdom could be that wisdom is intellectuality plus self-discipline plus purity of mind soiled with truth and love. At best, an intellectual has worldly wisdom but not spiritual wisdom. To develop a wholesome personality head (intellect), heart (mind) and hands (body) are to be co-opted, coordinated and harmonized. We should possess head as that of Shankara, heart as that of Buddha and hands as that of king Janaka.

The highest component of a man's personality is the *atma* which is basically the spiritual part of the personality. Soul is 90 per cent of a man's personality, even though 90 per cent people are not aware of this. Soul can be one's friend as well as enemy. Enemy when there is no integration of being with his soul. To reach the spiritual level, we have to transcend physical, mental and intellectual level of our personality. Transcendence means staying at the highest level but, at the same time, supplementing the lower levels of our personality. At the spiritual level, there is emphasis on inner purity, inner calmness, enlarged vision, equality, insight and intuition. At this level, we are least concerned about worldly desires and our sole desire, if we may call it a desire, is to get as close to the Divinity or the Ultimate Reality, while doing our best to contribute towards the well-being of society.

At the spiritual level, we develop an attitude that makes us to see bright side of things always and every time. We remain ever sincere and committed in whatever we do. We hate none and love all. As we raise our level of personality to the highest level, our attachment to lower things drops off automatically. This is true renunciation or *tyaga* which is not leaving something but getting hooked to the values of life. There is also a change of attitude at the spiritual level. There is no direct link between scholarship and spiritual wisdom as they are not one and the same. Scholarship is different from spiritual wisdom, though it can pave the way for it. Similarly, a man of spiritual wisdom may not be a scholar like Sri Ramakrishna. Spirituality gives enlightenment. Enlightenment is not an intellectual state. It is a state of spiritual awareness which comes through moral building.

Our energy levels also improve when we raise our level of personality. The more we lose ourselves in something bigger than us, the more energy shall we have. At the physical level, we only have physical energy. When we are at our mental level, our mind acquires strength which is more than what was available to us at the physical level. At the mental level, we transcend the limitations of physical body. At the intellectual level, we further energize ourselves, and at the spiritual level, our energy is the highest which enables us to live in constant cheer even against heavy odds. When we are at the spiritual level of our personality, there is nothing that we cannot achieve. Such is the intensity of spiritual energy that it makes a mute person speak and a lame person climb a mountain. In the old age, we may lose physical energy but this shortfall can be made up by acquiring more energy when we raise our level of personality to mental, intellectual and finally the spiritual level. Knowledge gives us energy. Food, sleep and our breath give us energy.

There is a thing called integrated personality which we gain by increasing goodness in us, by the rise of spiritual values in us. Integrated personality is that where all levels of our personality are available to us but under control of the spiritual level of our being. In integrated personality, there is a balance and harmony in our personality which is influenced by spirituality which manifest as honesty in our conduct. Freedom from dependence, fortitude, forbearance, equal vision and evenness of mind—all are created at different levels in us but controlled by our spiritual strength. When we possess an integrated personality, we are courteous, approachable and accessible. We give love and comfort to all who come in our contact. We do not shut ourselves from the world but we do our best to give something to it from our side. We also believe that every interaction which we have with others will teach us something. We live to learn and update ourselves. We also develop the ability to talk to every one irrespective of the difference in age and mental ability of people we come across. We come down from our spiritual level and speak to others who are at different planes of personality. Personality can also be defined in terms of distinctive qualities of a person which makes him socially attractive or a famous person or a celebrity. Hence, there is ever a need of integrating BMI complex and soul for achieving excellence in human behaviour.

Western philosophers describe human personality in their own way. According to Niccolo Machiavelli, an Italian philosopher, those who possess highest excellence think about others; the ones who try to understand the thinking of others possess excellence. But the ones who do not possess either of these two qualities are worthless. And those who have both these qualities are the best. German philosopher Friedrich Wilhelm Nietzsche held that unless you stop thinking about yourself, you cannot be great in the true sense. A western philosopher said that there are three types of human personality—Conformists, Criminals and Godly. Conformists are those who are intellectually oriented and Criminals are these who defy the laid down code. Then there are those who are morally upright and godly in essence. Greek philosopher Aristotle gave the example of a sports stadium to describe different types of personalities. There are those who are playing the game in the stadium and they are very few. These are the leaders and pathfinders. Then there are those who are watching the game. They are interested in the game being played in the stadium and have the ability to become future players if they try hard. Then there are hawkers in the stadium who are neither interested in those who are playing the game nor in those who are watching the game. They are only interested in selling their goods to the spectators. The third type of people are the average people who are only interested about themselves. They are the selfish type. Among those who are leaders or path-setters are American civil right activist Martin Luther King and Nelson Mandela of South Africa. They lived for others in the true spirit of what Albert Einstein said that only a life lived for others is a life worthwhile. On the Indian front, we have Mahatma Gandhi who was a mass leader. Swami Vivekananda lived to do good to others.

When we examine western concept of human personality, we find that it is not different or at variance with the Indian concept. The Indian way of looking at a human personality is that the lowest are those who are selfish, who think and act keeping their personal interest in mind. Then there are people who are not selfish but have a goal in life which they want to achieve. Then there are selfless people who are more concerned about welfare of others than their own. They are the best.

Spirituality helps us to integrate various components of our personality to achieve comprehensive wellness of body, mind and spirit. Mind gives us inner stability and peace. For developing one's personality, one must be fully aware of oneself. One should be fully aware of one's weaknesses so that they could be removed by one's strengths. Self-awareness is also called self-consciousness. You can develop your personality when there is no self-doubt. When you know yourself as you are, then you can try to improve your personality. By developing our personality, we do not have to become something special but remain an ordinary person who may be called extraordinary. We behold every person as ourselves and speak to them as if we are speaking to ourselves. It is as if you are looking at the mirror and talking to your own self. You require no special effort to do so if you have sense of inclusiveness and not exclusiveness. We should have a strong will to develop our personality, a will to follow the right path, and a will to discard the wrong path. The *Chandogya Upanishad* says that a man is primarily his will. As is his will so is his life and so does one become. Willpower enables us to break away from our substandard habits like selfishness and dishonesty. When man raises his level of consciousness, his will falls in line with the Divine will. When we attempt to rise above our limitations, we will succeed. To realize one's own reason is a step towards one's development.

Life is a battle between spirit and matter, knowledge and ignorance, self-control and temptation, and between discrimination and sensual life. When we attempt to fight this battle, our journey proceeds from humanness to divinity. Nature of a man consists of mental tendencies formed by the virtuous and evil acts of past lives as well as present life. They operate even in wise person in whom evil tendencies are very few.

Life is full of challenges, ups and downs, doubts and dualities. The world is also a battlefield for us. Nobody is going to give room to us. We have to make room for ourselves by showing our capabilities. Man has to fight two battles simultaneously: the inner ones and the outer ones. Out of these, the inner battle—the battle between the good and bad in us—is more important and a man must fight continuously. For those who are interested in personality development, the main battle is inner battle of life through which man overcomes weaknesses. An average person is more concerned about outer battle which he fights not necessarily on moral grounds as he considers fulfilment of worldly desires as the main purpose of life. He may become a worldly successful person but inwardly he is not successful. Worldly achievements may make a person great in the eyes of others but inwardly his personality is lacking. A worldly person is a selfish person who lives for his own sake in pursuit of short-lived gains. Rabindranath Tagore said that a man must live in largeness giving oneself to what is greater than himself, to ideas which are larger than his individual self, to the idea of his country, humanity and God. This holds good only for those who develop their personality to the highest level. Then one develops the ability to turn minuses into pluses and can face difficult situations and sail through them. A man is free in the real sense when he acts from the highest level of his personality and considers every situation in life as an opportunity for learning and growth. Outwardly, he is dynamic and vibrant and inwardly he is calm and composed.

In developing our personality, we must employ good means to secure good ends. Gandhiji stressed on good means which according to him would take care of good ends or good results. The western concept lays emphasis on good end without much concern on the quality of means employed to secure good results. But of late, India is following the western concept of securing good ends whereas the West is now paying attention towards the means. India unfortunately has a tendency to follow the West as most of us lack knowledge of our great spiritual heritage. Whatever happened in the West, say 20 years ago, is happening in India now. Today, the West is appreciating the Indian way of life but India continues to borrow from the West. We do not realize that if we borrow things which do not belong to the Indian way of life, they will harm us in the long run.

A developed personality is that where a man uses his head, heart and hands effectively in a coordinated and purposeful manner. Head or intellect inclined towards *atma* should guide the mind on how to deal with various situations in life. But the head does not deal with human values; these only come out from heart. Head may take you far in life but it is the heart, the reservoir of human values, which will make you reach the destination with good vibes all around. It is the heart which dictates you that you should love for love's sake. It is the heart which tells you to be kind for the sake of kindness. Some people say that we are good to others but others are not good to us. Why should we be good to people who are not good to us. That only shows that your love, goodness and kindness is conditional and when that is so, you will not progress inwardly. Therefore, make your kindness and love unconditional. You shall ever feel happy. Then you build your own support system without relying on others. This is how one should build up his personality. Follow the example of Buddha who remained good to others without bothering whether others returned goodness to him. Buddha never fished goodness from others. To use hands effectively means that one should work for the sake of work without looking for the results of one's actions. When you adopt this attitude, people will appreciate your work.

When we find that people we confront are indifferent towards morality and human behaviour, we should follow the advise given in the *Mahabharata* on how to deal with such people. It says that one should conquer anger of others by non-anger, evil of others by saintliness, conquer a miser by giving gifts to him and conquer the falsehood by truthfulness. No sin should be committed in retaliation of a sin.

When we love others and are loved by others, we elevate ourselves to newer heights. It is said that he who knows but does not love does not know. The reverse is also true. He who loves and does not know, does not love. Both head and heart need to be developed to know and love. Love wipes off differences between two men. Though divine love is the highest form of love it does not mean that human love is wrong. Human love need not be renounced but should be spiritualized without possessiveness or expectations. Through human love spiritual love is unfolded.

Love and Be Loved

In human heart, there is always a desire to love and be loved. To love others and be loved by others is akin to feeling sunshine from both sides, front as well as rear. Looks impossible but can be made possible. To love others is straightforward and needs no explanation. To get others love you, make yourself a person who is lovable, cared, valued and respected. To be loved by others cannot be demanded. Others would love you only if you have qualities that attract love. To truly love others means such a feeling should be devoid of a return love. When you insist that person you love should love you on the principle of reciprocity, you are being unfair to the concept of love. Irrespective of the love of others, you should love others like a mother loves her newborn child. It is love for love's sake. Only if you understand this will you be able to appreciate what true love means. The quickest way to receive love is to give it without expectations and continue giving it. When you remove your expectation in love, you start appreciating everything. Then your love does not depend on someone else.

Love according to Buddha does not mean an attachment to a person or object through which one hopes to satisfy his selfish cravings. Real love is endless self-immolation, compassion freely flowing towards all creation. Maharishi Ramana said that love yourself first before you love the world. It is because you can only give that to the world, which you yourself possess. Our capacity to love others depends upon our ability to love ourselves. We can only love ourselves when we outgrow our limitations. The biggest gain in loving yourself is that by doing so, you pay attention to evolve yourself at all levels of your personality—physical, emotional, psychological, intellectual and spiritual. Love is expansion: it is the only law of life. Love is listening to and respecting others. Buddha said that what is most needed is a loving heart. In whose heart love dwells, for him the whole world is a family. There is a Tibetan saying that many illnesses can be cured by love and compassion. Love removes hatred from our heart.

Loving yourself does not mean loving your ego or becoming selfish. Loving yourself means loving your own company and enjoying it to the core. There are a few tips which can incline a person to love oneself. The most important thing is to develop self-esteem which is to feel good about oneself, be honest to oneself and focus on positive traits of your personality. Many people confuse love with attachment. In attachment, your love is directed towards specific persons and not all, whereas in real love, you love one and all. Attachment contracts whereas love expands. When you grow inwardly in love, you would see love outside in the same way as a good person only sees goodness outside. To love oneself, one must shun all what is wrong inside us. To love oneself, one should give higher preference to upgrading oneself rather than upgrading one's belongings like car, clothes and house.

To love all, we must love others unconditionally. This love is genuine love where we have consideration and concern for welfare of all. It is a kind of radiation from our inner being. Unconditional love which is also called universal love is non-selective, non-personal but impersonal. In such love, you do not need physical presence or response from the person you love. In ordinary love, you fall in love which is not the case in universal love where you stand where you are. It is the love for the entire humanity. When Swami Vivekananda was asked how best we can serve others, his reply was by loving others. One way to know the meaning of universal love is to constantly wish for the well being of all. That which is universal is blissful. Universal love is never possessive. Possessiveness is bondage. To love all is not generosity but an inevitable necessity. When you talk to anyone with a lovable attitude, your talk will be impressionable. The person you talk to will tell you at the end of conversation, 'I felt good talking to you.' To love all, one has to imbibe a virtue of not seeing faults in others. Fault finding disturbs our peaceful disposition. Only when we are peaceful we can be happy.

The highest form of love is divine love. He who loves God knows God because God is love. God is easily available with love. When we love God truly and sincerely, our senses cease to exist and all our desires get merged in the love of God. There is never any boredom in divine love. In human love, people start with love but they may get bored with the passage of time. In divine love, one feels elevated since the excitement never dies. You are always in the process of raising yourself to greater heights.

Love which we know and express in the human plane is the reflection of divine love. The *Upanishads* tells us that the self is the dearest of all things and only through self is everything else dear. It is not for the sake of wife that wife is dear but it is for the sake of self. True fulfilment of love is possible only when we turn our love towards God. Love is like a river which when obstructed finds a new direction. The story of Savitri from the *Mahabharata* shows that pure genuine love can nullify the decree of fate and even triumph over death.

Love is the only medicine that can heal the wounds of the world. As body needs food to grow, soul needs love to manifest itself. There should be no trading in love. He who is filled with love is filled with God. Love must manifest its reality in deeds and not just in words. When one is filled with divine love, there is no space left in the mind to allow baser sentiments to enter. Divine love prepares ground for devotion (*bhakti*) which is much more than love.

Bhakti or devotional love is pure love untainted by selfishness. Though divine love is the highest form of love, it does not mean that there is something wrong in human love and that it should be avoided. Through human love, we develop compassion and caring attitude which is no less essential for our spiritual journey.

By all means, love your community, state and the country, but your love should not restrict to the borders of your community, state and country. It should encompass the entire universe and creation. It is sometimes said that worldly love is like an ocean which has a bottom whereas spiritual love is like a sky which has no limits. Spiritual love is the highest and is always above self, whereas worldly love can be selfish where one looks for one's own comfort zone.

As stated above a silent mind is desirable for personality development. What does silence mean? Does it mean only keeping quiet or has it got a wider connotation? We shall try to analyse this.

Silence is Essential for Self-Perfection

In the *Bhagavad Gita,* Lord Krishna states, "Of all the secrets I am silence." In the *Upanishads,* silence has been described as a means to know God. The *Upanishads* say, "Silence is *Brahman,* Ultimate Reality is *Brahman* and *Atma* is Pure Silence. Ultimate Reality being beyond speech, Silence is the only way of expressing it." It is well known that silence plays a vital role in one's spiritual growth. In silence, one goes deep into the inner core of one's personality to feel the spark of God within. A silent mind is a meditative mind. It generates new ideas. In prayers, you speak to God; in Silence, God speaks to you. The greatest minds are silent minds. Silence develops willpower, conserves energy and makes one creative. Silence is to mind what sleep is to body. Silence energizes the mind. It is the austerity of mind. External silence can be achieved by making one's room sound proof. But what is more important is inner silence where one becomes refined inwardly. In a conversation, when you are silent, you are listening to others and getting opportunities which you lose while you are talking. Listening helps one to gain knowledge and achieve silence. Listening also gives a message that I care for you. Listening contributes almost 50 per cent of effective conversation. Silence does not mean physical inertness; it is an active experience where power of intuition unfolds. Silence is also a means to avoid confrontation. It teaches you to meditate where you summon all energies to one idea and convert your observation into vision. When a man completes his journey from words to silence, he is on his way to enlightenment. Swami Vivekananda said, "Out of purity and silence comes the word of power."

Silence is another way to give an answer. When Buddha was asked if God existed, he maintained silence. The questioner then told Buddha that his silence meant that God does not exist. Buddha said, "I did not say that," and again maintained silence. By remaining silent, Buddha avoided any metaphysical discussion, which according to him, was not necessary for one's progress in life. That is why silence is regarded as greater than speech. When one goes deep into silence, one does not even think. This is also a form of Yoga. Patanjali defined silence as cessation of thinking principle. Christianity advised man to be still to know 'I am God'. Silence gives calmness, peace and stillness which are aids to purify mind. Calmness like sleep refreshes you. Silence supersedes hatred and harsh words, destroys anger and at the same time increases our faith in God. A mystic poet said, "I searched Him on hills and mountains but He was not found. But when I looked inside in silence, I found him."

Some of our saints like Maharishi Ramana, Vinoba Bhave and Sri Aurobindo practised silence for long spells even after they attained perfection. Maharishi Ramana is described as an epitome of silence. He taught *vichara marg* or path of self-enquiry (Who Am I), which can only be practised in Silence. In the *Upanishads,* there is a beautiful episode to underscore the importance of silence. A disciple asks his teacher to tell him about *Brahman*. The teacher maintains silence instead of giving a reply. When the disciple repeats his question, but the teacher maintains silence again. Not satisfied, the disciple asks the teacher for the third time but the teacher again maintains silence. Now, the disciple realizes that the nature of *Brahman* is unthinkable and unexplainable and so he does not repeat his question again. But instead, he practises silence and finds an answer to his query. Mark Twain said that the less a man knows, the bigger the noise he makes.

To practise silence, one must observe silence for sometime during the day. First, practise silence in words, even though when the mind is not quiet. Another way of practising silence of words is to carry out a day-to-day assessment of yourself in your mind. Try to speak as little as possible, avoiding unnecessary conversation. Also remember that whatever you speak should exhibit the quality of your mind. Develop a habit of reading; it automatically silences you. One should learn the art of holding the words in the mouth if they are of little consequence. The golden rule is to listen more and talk less. Silence is a great virtue. It avoids unnecessary discussions and disputes. Silence is not just closing your lips and abstaining from talking. It is much more than that. Real silence is when you have silenced your passions, desires, attachment and ill feelings. True silence means total self-transformation of oneself.

Enlightened people require speech to spread knowledge and goodness all around. If such people observe long spells of silence, it will not be useful to the humanity because it would be deprived of wisdom. For instance, if Swami Vivekananda had observed silence for a long time, the world would have missed some of his greatest lessons on the *Vedanta* and human behaviour. When you know something which would be beneficial to the society, break silence and let others know it.

> *Men acquire a particular quality by constantly acting a particular way. You become just by performing just actions, temperate by performing temperate actions, brave by performing brave actions.*
>
> ***Aristotle***

Morality and Personality

The Roots of Violence: *Wealth without work, Pleasure without conscience, Knowledge without character, Commerce without morality, Science without humanity, Worship without sacrifice, Politics without principles.*

Mahatma Gandhi

Morality and Ethics

While money comes and goes, morality comes and grows. To be moral is to follow righteousness and accepted norms of social behaviour. To be moral also means possessing good character. For a truly moral person, everyone is equal. He is humane and recognizes dignity of man on the basis of human values. So how does one define value? Value is that which does greatest good to the greatest number.

Victory often comes from moral courage. When one follows moral code of conduct, one makes his life perfect, comprehensive and universal. All religions lay down moral code of conduct which their followers are expected to understand and internalize.

Ethics is the science of morality. All moral laws are not universal as they may vary in respective communities due to certain historical, economical and geographical compulsions. But some moral laws have universal significance at all times and when they acquire such status, they become ethics. Thus, ethics can be defined as morality plus universal acceptance. Truth, non-violence, peace, harmony, love, compassion, righteousness and forgiveness which have universal acceptance fall within the purview of ethics. It is said that great men are not those who have money and health but are those who are morally and ethically upright. Vinobha Bhave, a scholar, thinker and writer went to the extent of saying that a country should be defended not by arms but by ethical behaviour. Emperor Ashoka said what matters in life is not personal status or position, but a man's virtues and values. Acharya Tulsi from Jainism who is running a movement of morality called 'Anuvrata' says that until people of a nation are moral, political freedom cannot serve the purpose.

There is an erosion of ethical standards despite the fact that India has a spiritual, religious and inward looking philosophical culture. There are a number of causes due to which our countrymen are living below morality life (BML). One of these is a decisive increase in the expectations of people, resulting in unrelenting increase in wants as distinct from needs. When wants are not met within the means, people resort to unfair means to enhance their income, giving a boost to corruption and dishonesty. The tendency seems to be rising due to consumerism that encourages instinctive desires with no sense of reason and morality. Our *Upanishads* say that when a man prospers, gains what appears desirable, or even conquers enemy, he perishes at the roots. Somehow, we wrongly feel that if our desires are met, we can be happy forever. Such thinking arises out of ignorance and self-centeredness. This is not right since the main aim of life is certainly not the pursuit of material happiness.

Material happiness is temporary; it never lasts. Material life gives us ordinary life where mind follows senses and senses follow material objects giving momentary happiness. Real and everlasting happiness comes when a man looks inwards. It comes when he acquires moral virtues. The more we look within and understand ourselves, the more happy we would be. When we are one with the Divine, we are one with the whole stream of life.

Besides corruption, there are other things also which are lowering our level of morality. First and foremost, we are lacking in self-discipline. Self-discipline is not a matter of intelligence. It is a matter of will and willpower. Willpower comes from right thinking and right actions. Next, we are not obedient. We do not realize that social order depends on obedience to authority. Indians by nature do not like to respect authority. When we do not like to obey, we can never learn to command respect from others. Swami Vivekananda's view that you first learn to serve and over a period of time you will automatically become a leader seems to have been lost on people. We like fault finding. But we do not like to accept our own faults. We tend to focus on negatives of others rather than the positives which all of us have in some proportion. On the other hand, we are too good in blaming others. Then by and large, we are not sincere and committed to our duties. Insincerity and dishonesty are the biggest problems facing us.

Our work culture is considered to be below par as we are lacking in team spirit. Lack of team spirit causes a drop in the collective IQ of a nation. We are more concerned about our rights than our responsibilities and duties. We do not realize that when we undertake our responsibilities sincerely, rights and privileges will automatically follow. Those who look for their rights are weak and those who accept and discharge their responsibilities and duties sincerely without being concerned about their rights are strong.

India might be moving ahead with the world in scientific and technical advances but it is lagging behind in moral and spiritual growth. If India needs any kind of revolution, it is spiritual revolution based on education. The spiritual revolution is an inward movement directed towards the higher values of life.

Let us try to understand if by raising the level of personality one can overcome the major problems faced by India. First on the list is corruption which is widespread and has become a social disorder in our society. The root cause of the spread of corruption is dishonesty and moral deterioration. Most of us have now become indifferent to it and accept it as an inevitable occurrence. Lack of transparency and accountability also encourages corruption. Our procedures and systems are complicated and attract a corrupt mind.

Any amount of teaching will be of little use until an individual himself rises above corruption. He has to ask himself "Am I dishonest and corrupt?" We as individuals are the means and society is the end. Every individual has to fight corruption and dishonesty at his own level before turning to eradicate corruption from the society. Corruption cannot be uprooted overnight; it has to be phased out with everyone's efforts. Transparency in public dealings helps in removing suspicion from people's mind about the working of any organization. For this to happen, people holding top positions in government and other establishments have to set the trend by becoming corruption-free themselves, and thus providing inspiration down the ladder.

Apart from all other measures, we must also develop a will to fight corruption. Willpower is something which a person generates within himself and applies it to complete his task. To be moral is to possess a strong will. Success comes from right actions and to perform right actions we must have a right will. Our successes and failures depend upon the strength of our will. Willpower can also be defined as a positive and creative function of mind which empowers a person to do desired actions in a definite way and avoid undesirable ones, even though they may be tempting. We do wrong because our willpower is weak. Sometimes we do wrong since the whole society is doing wrong. This thinking is due to our weak willpower which gets influenced by the will of the majority. Sometimes even majority may not be right. Willpower gives us the freedom to choose. We should never allow our will to be weakened by our bad habits and worldly attractions. Our character is based on our habits and if our habits are wrong, our character becomes unrighteous and this weakens our willpower.

Now, we come back to one of the chief reasons for spread of corruption. This is insincerity. We are not sincere by nature. Sincerity in true sense means aligning our thoughts, words and deeds towards the same goal. Sincerity gives us strength, patience and success. It means to be committed to the task in hand. When a person is sincere, he is bound to reach his goal. Sincerity and integrity complement each other. When we possess integrity, we also have sincerity and vice versa. The simplest way to develop sincerity is to be truthful at all times which would align our thoughts, words and actions. A sincere person will act on what he thinks and on what he says whereas an insincere person will think something, say something else, and act completely differently from both. Enlightened people act on what they think and say, whereas ordinary people do not follow this simple rule of action.

Our work culture needs improvement. Selfless work is a means to develop our personality. What the *Bhagavad Gita* calls skill in action is nothing but our efficiency in action. By efficient work, we enrich human life and remove corruption, poverty, violence, crime and backwardness from society. Work is an inseparable part of our life. It is an important means for our self-evolution. Our scriptures describe selfless work as a meeting point between God and Man. It is through work only that we can improve our world as well as inner life. But unfortunately, we work enthusiastically only when we have some personal interest in the work we undertake.

Mahatma Gandhi once said that the main trouble with Indians is that they prefer to sit idle. Almost similar views were expressed by Swami Vivekananda when he said that the basic problem with Indians is that they do not like to work. Pandit Jawahar Lal Nehru said that Indians are lazy not only with hands and feet but also intellectually. They prefer to stick to the beaten track instead of giving new ideas to improve the quality of work. How true is this statement even today! We do not like any change in the existing system because change involves fresh thinking in which we are not interested since it means some extra work for us. It is a fact that we suffer from some serious faults like hypocrisy and non-obedience, and we argue to find a way out to protect ourselves.

Indians do not follow the dictum of working for work's sake. We do not accept that work is to be taken as duty irrespective of the type of work. When we accept our work as our duty, we shall never be tired or bored in doing it. What prompts us to work is some sort of incentive like 'If I get that I will do this'. Incentive is the lowest rung of the ladder that attracts man to work. Still better is when one is motivated to work. And the best is when one is inspired to work, which is the highest rung of the work ladder. So, if one wants to achieve excellence in doing something, he should be driven from within. Inspiration always comes from within. Inspiration is not motionless, it is a vibration. It is received from a higher source. When we are inspired, we are prepared to work even at the cost of our personal discomfort. So, many times people commit to others but fail to fulfill it because the person to whom they commit does not matter to them. Then there are some other type of people who work when someone is watching them. They prefer to avoid work if they are not supervised.

The doctrine of selfless work or *karma yoga* as described in the *Bhagavad Gita* originated from our country. It defines *karma yoga* as efficiency in work. Efficiency in work is obtained by sincerity and honesty. Such work is always skillful. In other words, spiritual advancement is directly proportional to selfless performance of one's duty. The *Bhagavad Gita* further says that one who performs his duty without any personal interest attains the maximum. The efficient performance of work not only becomes a means for our worldly welfare but it also contributes towards our development, provided the work is done honestly, sincerely and without caring to appease others, or in other words, without caring for the results of the work undertaken.

Efficiency in work gives productive efficiency at outer level and spiritual advancement within. We may be a clerk or a teacher; it makes no difference to our inner development. A person reduces himself to pettiness by his own thinking. The work does not ask you to slip into a *yogi's* garb. Rather it asks you to become a *karma yogi* by bringing about the change within; by accepting work as your duty. Rituals and priests fade away into the background when you rightly understand to discharge your duties. We must inject this 'duty idea' in our minds to improve our work performance. The *Bhagavad Gita* says that failing in one's duty is sin. Of late, the western management gurus are attempting to enrich themselves with the supremacy of action as laid down in the *Bhagavad Gita*.

People give a number of reasons for our below par work culture. Some point out that India that remained invaded for centuries will take its own time to develop a positive attitude towards dedication. Others say that the extreme climatic condition in India is not conducive to efficient functioning. These reasons do not seem to carry much conviction. Our efficient performance of work does not depend on the external conditions we are placed in but on our inner motive behind the work. We tend to work mechanically and do not pay attention to train our minds while on work.

Who will take the lead to improve our work culture? At the individual level, we all will have to put in our best to set aside our attitude of being. Besides, heads of organizations and educational institutes have to set personal examples by playing a pivotal role in bringing about efficiency in work. It would also be necessary to hold periodical discussions and lectures on how to improve the quality of work. The *karma yoga* of the *Bhagavad Gita* would particularly be useful and should be taught to one and all. It is pertinent to note that certain portions of this epic are being taught at the educational institutes in the West.

Work is our greatest teacher. When we work efficiently, we get an opportunity for self-understanding and self-expression besides self-development. Efficient and selfless work builds up our capacity for team work and it also binds us to the society we live in. There is no other choice but to make the best of our abilities. We must work in a spirit of sacrifice or *yajna* which means that our work should benefit others on the principle of equality. When we improve our work culture and understand the 'duty idea' in work, we acquire self-discipline and concentrate on our work rather than on the negativity of others. When we work selflessly, there is an overall improvement in our character.

It is rightly said that if life in general is to be made decent and dignified, ethics must control social life. Indian tradition lays down 26 virtues which are listed in the *Bhagavad Gita*. These need to be practised and internalized in order to have a perfect personality. When we are morally sound, we develop an all inclusive sound personality. And when our personality is fully developed, we give compliments to others rather than fishing compliments from them.

Out of the virtues listed in the *Bhagavad Gita*, 10 are considered to be the most crucial. These are Truthfulness, Non-violence, Fearlessness, Forgiveness, Absence of hatred, Self-control, Charity, Renunciation, Peacefulness and Study of scriptures. Virtues are reflected by intent and not appearance.

Truthfulness

Truthfulness holds the key to self-perfection. Everything comes and goes except the truth. When truth is known, every doubt in the world disappears. Truth can never remain hidden; sooner or later, it will come out. Unfortunately, many of us feel that truth is bitter. But is it really so? Truth is certainly bitter to those who live on the foundation of falsehood. Such people fear the truth and call it bitter, but for those who lead a righteous life, truth is a source of strength.

All religions and their scriptures value truth to its utmost and define it in many ways. *Brahman* or Ultimate Reality is described as truth in the *Upanishads*. Truth is God and final bliss. *Ekam sat viprah bahudha vadant* (The Truth is one; the wise call it by many names). *Satyameva Jayate* (Truth alone triumphs) is the national motto of India. Truthfulness in thoughts, words and deeds is the fundamental requirement of one's evolution. The *Bhagavad Gita* upholds this when it says that one should rise above different modes of nature or *prakriti* and establish oneself in truth. Sri Ramakrishna said that if a man clings to truth, he would ultimately realize God.

Truth is like a compass that shows you the right track. Truth is God, God is truth, God is love and God is beauty. So truth is also love and beauty. The *Mahabharata* says that there is no virtue equal to truth and there is no sin greater than falsehood. To be truthful means a prior commitment to non-violence. Non-violence is the basis for search of truth, said Mahatma Gandhi. Let my voice rule not by violence but by evidence of things. The *Vedanta* declares that truth must be free from contradictions, so evident that it can do without any proof. Truth must be universal in the broadest sense. Swami Vivekananda exhorted that nothing but going towards truth of reality will make you strong. *The Bible* says that you shall know the truth and truth shall make you free. What a beautiful statement is this! When we know the truth, all our doubts and misconceptions fade away and things become crystal clear. Abraham Lincoln once said that 'I am nothing but truth and truth is everything'.

Truth is the guiding principle for both worldly and spiritual life. Path to excellence can be laid by truth alone. Human relations can never thrive on untruth. Love of truth also raises us beyond sense perceptions. Dr Radhakrishnan said that truth can never be pursued except by those who are in love with goodness. It is generally seen that as one grows in position and status in worldly life, he distances himself from the truth. I have often noticed that quiet a large number of high-ranked worldly people are found expressing strong opinion on morality-related issues as if they hold key to wisdom. They may have some knowledge of moral values but they surely lack wisdom which is only obtained by practising the moral values which most of them do not. People may also listen to them, but their knowledge on moral values being hearsay and not experienced, it would not penetrate into the minds of those who are being addressed. The point I am raising is that can one teach morality to others without being morally upright himself? My answer is a big NO. It is like telling others to live truthfully without living truthfully oneself. Preaching morality without practice is always ineffective. Real teachers are those who teach by personal example. First walk the talk yourself and then talk to others.

Non-violence

Truth and non-violence are considered as two sides of the same coin. Gandhiji said that unless you are truthful, you cannot be non-violent, and unless you are non-violent, you cannot be truthful. The 20th Century is referred to as the century of violence. It witnessed two world wars in which millions of people died and many more injured. If we do not control violence, 21st Century will be more vulnerable to violence since we now live in an overcrowded and polluted world in which people have a very low level of tolerance.

Violence does not only mean killing or hurting living beings. Violence also means quarrelling, fighting, criticizing, backbiting and condemning others. To hurt the feelings of others is also violence. Female foeticide is violence of the worst form. Dishonesty in financial matters is also a form of violence. Even suicide is an act of violence. Acts which are not righteous end up in violence. Violence is like a cancer. It silently eats away from within. A society that tolerates violence or a nation that is built on perpetrating violence on others anywhere anytime is on the way to destruction. Violence leads to poverty and poverty to lack of education. Illiteracy is the mother of all ills of our society. Violence breeds and feeds on violence. Manifestations of violence in various forms would make one easily conclude that we are living on a planet which is full of violence.

There is structural violence where social, political and cultural structures oppress, segregate, exclude or marginalize groups of people. There is economic violence where economic life is so organized that it denies the basic needs of people. Social violence exists where people are excluded on the basis of colour, gender, caste and ethnicity. There is also domestic violence where women are abused and treated brutally. Psychological violence is where people are deprived of dignity and made to live in fear. Moral violence is where people living in the society are denied human rights. Then there is violence which arises out of jealousy, fear and hatred. Sage Mahavira said that as long as there is inequality in society, violence cannot be totally uprooted. However, unnecessary violence should be curbed. He also said that violence results from attachment to our possessions.

Can one overcome violence or come out of violence? Is there a way out of violence? This is possible if one can practise non-violence. There are three ways to practise non-violence–physical, verbal and mental. Practising physical non-violence means respect for others' life as we respect our own. In verbal non-violence, one should not treat others with harsh words. Mental non-violence demands that we should think good about others. Complete non-violence is total absence of ill will against others. We are truly spiritual when we are totally non-violent with a heart filled with love and compassion. To avoid violence, we should accept others as they are. We should also improve our personal behaviour and acquire a forgiving attitude.

As far as possible, we should live a simple life. Simplicity is antidote for violence. Simplicity is not a life of poverty but it is a life of purpose. Simplicity has more to do with the state of mind than a person's possessions. When we choose to lead a simple life, we place high priority on the quality and integrity of our relationship with every other aspect of life—with ourselves, other people, creatures, the earth and the universe.

Non-violence can also be inculcated by reading stories of preachers of non-violence. We must also acquaint others with non-violent personalities such as Lord Mahavira, Ashoka, Buddha, Mahatma Gandhi, Mother Teresa and Dalai Lama. All religions of the world support non-violence at the core of their teachings. The *Bhagavad Gita* says that one should treat all beings like oneself. Other religions also convey the same idea in different words like: Do not do unto others what you do not want others to do unto you. When you want people to be good to you, then you cannot possibly be bad to them. You have no choice but to be good to others. If you love non-violence, you should become non-violent yourself. This is what Gandhiji meant by saying, "Be the change you want to see in the world."

India is identified in the world as a country that has practised non-violence or *ahimsa* as its spirit. The concept of non-violence was first born here itself and rose to form the core of Indian morality. Ours being a multi-ethnic and multi-religious society, it is imperative that we resolve all differences in a peaceful manner. The *Mahabharata* extols non-injury as the highest dharma of the world. The scripture also asks, 'How can he who wants to live kill others?' King Ashoka said that non-violence alone triumphs and not violence. We have exported the doctrine of non-violence to other countries but are failing to prevent violence that still exists in our country. We are not as sensitive to the needs of others as we are to our own. We must impart peace education to our people, and introduce the same in our educational system. Non-violence may not work at times but violence never works.

Peace Education

Peace is a way of life and not a subject as such. Peace education means teaching students to resolve conflicts within and outside. Peace should be dealt under two heads: peace for all, that is living in a stress free environment, and learning to maintain peace. Peace education means learning about peace and learning for peace. Learning about peace means obtaining knowledge and understanding of what contributes to peace and what disturbs it. Peace education means learning the skills, attitude and values that contribute to peace. Peace education should be treated as a part of value education. We must end all forms of violence including discrimination on the basis of birth.

Fearlessness

In the enumeration of divine qualities in The *Bhagavad Gita*, Lord Krishna said fearlessness comes on top of the list. Fearlessness is its central message. Our *Upanishads* repeatedly emphasize fearlessness. The *Bhagavad Gita* says that where there is knowledge, there is fearlessness. By placing the quality of fearlessness at the top of the list of divine attributes, it emphasizes that a fearless person alone can become perfect and spiritually awakened. It also says that a doubting mind is a fearful mind.

Only knowledge can remove doubts; only wisdom can remove ignorance. Wisdom and fear are opposed to each other. If there is fear, there is no wisdom, and if there is wisdom, there is no fear. They cannot coexist in the same body.

We are afraid of many things: of sufferings, of punishment if we wrong others, of the world if we are weak-willed, of death and at times of our own self. We are so obsessed with the idea of fear that we brand a morally upright person as a God-fearing person. Such labelling is incorrect because a morally upright person is God-loving and not God-fearing. In the initial stage of our journey towards God, we may be God-fearing but as we advance on the spiritual path, we become God-loving. Lord Rama said that those who seek my protection, I give them fearlessness from all beings. Fear is experienced by most of us even if we are well placed in life. Out of fear, the Aryans worshipped devas—the shining ones like Indra, Varuna and Surya—and set the trend of ritualistic practices. They were afraid of life hereafter and performed *yajnas* to attain heaven after death.

In the twists and turns of life, a new problem arises every now and then seeking attention and calling for a resolution. But if we are not alert or thoughtful, we will develop a sort of fear in deciding as to what should be the right course of action. The flow of life is unpredictable and such situations are bound to arise which will cause undue fear if not handled properly.

Ignorance is the major cause of fear. Non-apprehension or misapprehension of reality frightens a man. In both cases, the mind gets confused and cannot assert itself in a purposeful manner.

When ignorance is removed by acquiring knowledge, the element of fear starts receding. So we can safely say that knowledge alone is the antidote to fear. Most of our fears are self-created due to our limited thinking. Sometimes we fail to apply our mind in totality in a given situation. This creates a feeling of incompleteness within and attracts a fear of the unknown. It is well said that half the fear is baseless and the other half discreditable. When our thinking is rational, we are bound to eliminate fear from within. A rational mind does not entertain more than one idea at a time and the mind becomes unifocussed. Freedom from fear would also depend upon the environmental and social conditions around us and our capacity to handle them. If the outer conditions show no signs of improvement, then one has to strengthen the capacity to withstand them to counter fear. A fearful person does not hear his inner voice and is guided mostly by what others say. He loses his own convictions. He hesitates to undertake adventurous tasks. He develops a trend to run away from life and life becomes boring for him. Fear then becomes the biggest enemy in a man's evolutionary process. If we have fear, we are a coward, a slave and cannot attain freedom of thoughts, speech and action.

So, how can we deal with our biggest enemy called fear? The Hindu or the Vedantic view of life declares that God is within us. God is our guide, our guru, our friend. In our highest state of consciousness, we are co-partners of God in all cosmic activities. When we visualize God in all human beings, we shall be fearful of none. To combat fear, one should not give expression to fear even if it enters one's mind. Clarity of thought weakens fear. We should destroy fear by the power of our will. Filling up mind with powerful and positive ideas do not permit fear to enter our mind.

There are a few positive aspects of fear as well and these need to be recognized for better understanding of how it shapes our personality. It guards against danger. Sri Sri Ravi Shankar says that fear is essential to preserve orderliness in the world. Fear of death preserves life, fear of wrong maintains right, fear of sickness encourages us to remain healthy and fear of misery makes one adhere to righteousness. If at all we have to fear something, we should fear our immoral inclinations till they are thrown out and replaced by virtues. Fear at times shows good preparedness. While undertaking an examination good students often complain of fear. Those who are not serious do not complain. But those who complain are also the ones who get good grade. Positive fear about an issue will come only when you go a little deep into something. Good students demonstrating fear is an example of positive fear.

Forgiveness

We all make mistakes in life and we expect others to overlook them. But when others behave awkwardly with us, we are quick to react and are not inclined to forgive and forget the doings of others. Only when we forgive others for their mistakes, we should expect them to forgive us. We should always forgive others because we ourselves may be in need of forgiveness from others. Therefore, we must develop a forgiving attitude in life.

Forgiveness is a virtue, a divine trait and an act of graciousness. Forgiveness brings peace of mind. It brings about expansion in one's thinking and makes mind pure since it has a cleansing effect. We should forgive others unasked and stop blaming or being angry with them. All of us experience that people do hurt us in some proportion with their words and deeds. Such memories lie hidden in us and manifest sometimes whenever we see or hear about those who have annoyed us. The reason is that while we have forgiven them to some extent, we have not totally forgotten their ill deeds which have left some impression on our subconscious mind. Therefore, forgiving to be meaningful must end in forgetting. Real forgiving is not just saying—'I forgive you'—but it is an integrated act of forgiving and forgetting. This establishes inherent interconnectedness between forgiving and forgetting. Some people say that they have forgiven but they talk about the event with bitterness.

Forgiveness finds its full expression when those who forgive are strong mentally as well as physically. Hence it can be said that forgiveness is a weapon of strong. It should not be a symbol of weakness. Similar views were held by Gandhiji who said that forgiveness is the attitude of the strong, since the weak can never forgive. He further said that if all those who were wronged took revenge, it would mean an eye for an eye, which in turn would turn the whole world blind.

All religions testify that we should forgive. All religions of the world preach that we should not take any retaliatory action when harmed by others. According to Hinduism, forgiveness is the way to happiness. A wise man will always forgive. The *Bhagavad Gita* says that those who forgive are dear to God. According to a Hindu mythological tale, Saint Bhrigu hit Lord Vishnu with his foot because Lord Vishnu did not pay any attention to him when he called on Him. Lord Vishnu not only did not retaliate but even asked the saint if his foot was hurt in the process of hitting. This is an excellent example of non-retaliation when provoked which is tantamount to the act of forgiveness. Islam says that God Himself being forgiving loves those who forgive their fellow beings.

Forgiveness is one of the crucial teachings of all religions. Jesus Christ represents forgiveness. When Christ was being nailed to the cross, He said, "Father, forgive them because they do not know what they do." In '*The Sermon on The Mount*', Jesus asked us to be merciful so as to forgive. Buddhism teaches us not to wound anybody who is the cause of our suffering. Jainism advises mankind that one should not hold any ill will towards man, beast and even plant. Forgive all and be not revengeful, 'Forget and Forgive', and 'Live and Let Live' are the major teachings of Jainism. Sikhism states that countless people have perished without the spirit of forgiveness. It asks you to remove malice from your heart and treat the whole world as your friend. Similarly, other religions like Judaism, Confucianism and Shintoism also ask their followers to forgive. While Shintoism preaches to forgive others, it also asks adherents not to forgive oneself for one's ill behaviour. This underscores that one should mend oneself if one has offended others. Forgiveness does not mean condoning wrong behaviour of others. Forgiveness is an understanding when you do not take revenge from the person who has harmed you. Forgiveness is a man's understanding in dealing with others.

Attitude of forgiveness develops when one acquires an expanded consciousness and a broad outlook. A narrow-minded person can never forgive. Forgiveness becomes natural to a person who possesses qualities like self-control, non-violent attitude, peaceful state of mind, compassion, tolerance and forbearance. Forgiveness is the end result of a value-oriented life. When one has compassion, one shall be inclined to become friend of all with a loving attitude. When one possesses poise and equilibrium, he would be tolerant towards annoying attitude of others which shall indirectly make him a forgiving person. Yet another way of acquiring forgiveness is to live in the present and not revisiting the past. If you live in the past, old unfavourable memories will haunt you which can turn you revengeful. That is why our sacred books advise us not to relive the past but live in the present while concentrating on a significant goal. When you live in the present, you unload all ill memories of past including harm done to us by others. The *Bhagavad Gita* exhorts us to develop same sightedness while looking at a well-wisher, a friend, an enemy and also a hateful person. This is possible when we accept others as an extension of our own self on the basis of understanding that each one of us has the same divine principle within us.

Total materialist approach of the mankind towards life has made people selfish to the extent that they do not hesitate to trouble others for personal gains. When we have a revengeful attitude, it would keep our mind disturbed which would affect our efficiency. The *Bhagavad Gita* gives a solution to this when it says that a true *yogi* is not only the one who does not give trouble to others but also the one who is not troubled by others. When you are established in your inner self, ill behaviour of others directed towards you will not affect you. This is also termed as an act of forgiveness. A prayer highlights forgiveness as follows, "May all living beings grant me forgiveness. May I grant forgiveness to all so that we may all live in peace." Forgiveness also means universal friendship.

Absence of Hatred

The *Isha Upanishad* tells us that he who sees his own self in all beings cannot hate anyone by virtue of this understanding: He alone can love. Where there is hatred, there is no spiritual growth as hatred is a non conductor of spiritual energy. Hatred is also a subtle form of violence. Hatred develops from a sense of secretiveness. When we realize the all-pervading nature of God, a feeling of compassion comes into existence which removes hatred from our hearts. Hatred is as bad as attachment.

We love some, while others we do not. We do not mind saying 'I hate you' to the latter. Hatred disturbs one's peace of mind and also physical health when one raises the level of hatred to its highest. Hatred may also lead to violence. All men in this world are not identical. There shall be some who would be more intelligent and powerful than you. There should be some who have a better status than you or more money than you. So, when we start comparing ourselves with others, we may find some superior than us leading us to a feeling of dislike for them. This dislike for others can also arise when people do not agree to your views. Then we also have a tendency to find faults with others or speak ill of them. This pollutes our mind as a result of which we see nothing good in them. When this practice becomes a habit, we develop a sort of hatred for those we do not like. Another reason for developing hatred for others is that we keep our minds closed and refuse to accommodate others in our scheme of things. We do not like to share with others. Hatred lowers ourselves in our own eyes whereas love raises us, enlarges our vision and makes us a better person. Love for all and hatred for none is the central teaching of all scriptures. The *Bhagavad Gita* says that one should not hate anything. It asks us to adopt an equal vision which should remain so even towards a hateful person.

How do we rid ourselves of the hatred that we develop for others? First and foremost, we must develop in us an attitude of love towards all, friends as well as strangers, and see others as an extended self of our own. We can only love all when we have developed within us a feeling of equality and sameness towards others. We have to transcend duality or pairs of opposite, such as like and dislike, and attachment and aversion. Then we must acquire an ability to see good in everyone. It is easy to catch someone's bad traits because you do not require any distinct ability for that. But to see good things of others requires one to become good oneself first. If you hate anyone, nine out of ten times, it is due to your limited vision. A man who has malice towards others loses the power to see God in all, which is a reality, as the same spark of good is present in each of us.

Not hating others should be practised by everyone. The surest way to throw out hatred from your mind is to develop an eye to see something good in every person whom you meet. This way you will acquire abundance of goodness in your heart which would replace hatred. Our scriptures describe the world as a tree with large branches which represent human kind. In the light of this analogy, hating someone is as harmful as cutting that branch of the tree where you are sitting yourself. The *Bhagavad Gita* says that if anyone has hatred towards any creature, he cannot attain good. We are only accepted by God if we love all and hate none. Buddha said that hatred does not cease by hatred but only by love. This is the eternal rule.

Self-control

Self-control is one of the main virtues of life. Self-control gives peace, purity and ultimately bliss since it removes desire from our mind. Those who can control their mind can control others' mind as well. Self-realization is not possible for a person who lacks self-control. Control of senses is regarded as the highest *siddhi* (achievement) that a man can possess in his spiritual evolution. One who has mastered his senses can be called a sage. Temptations in life play havoc in one's spiritual advancement. Highly learned men and gifted people can also yield to temptations like the most unlearned and ignorant. A person who has not restrained his senses cannot be rescued from sinful acts. Self-control may start with self-denial but its deeper meaning is beyond it.

A man of self-control is a cultured man. He imposes restrictions on himself but there is a joy in it. Self-control is self-restraint and not forcible negation of senses. Self-control is more of disciplining yourself through a regulated way of living. A person who has control over his senses acquires freedom of thoughts, words and actions. He acquires the ability to work at his own will. Our scriptures say, "Do not be that *yogi* who reads holy books or wear saffron robes or someone who smears himself with sacred ash. Be a true *yogi* who has perfect control over his senses."

The *Bhagavad Gita* highlights the necessity of controlling the senses for self-evaluation. It says that when a person withdraws all the senses from the objective world and turns his mind inwards, he becomes a *Sthitaprajna*, that is, a man of steady wisdom. It admits that the turbulent sense forcibly leads astray the mind of even the struggling wise person. It suggests a remedy when Lord Krishna says that even though mind is restless and hard to control, yet by practice and dispassion mind can be controlled. A man of self-control attains knowledge and supreme peace. A rejection of senses is not as significant as the need to restrain them while interacting with various agencies.

In the fast moving world of today, how can we control our senses particularly when things around us are attracting us in sense indulgence? One thing which should be clearly understood is that self-control cannot be practised in isolation. Unless a person has awareness of higher values of life, he cannot be freed from the captivity of sense objects. Self-control does not mean self-suppression. Self-control is attained by filling the mind with higher values which results in dropping off lower impulses. For example, when the stomach is full with food, it does not tempt us to look at attractive items of food. Similarly, when our mind is filled with good thoughts, no appetite for worldly attractions remains.

An inclination towards a value-based life is necessary for obtaining success in self-control. Meditation is a good discipline for acquiring self-control. Self-control is attainable by self-awareness, self-analysis, self-introspection, self-inquiry, self-examination and self-criticism. When a person knows his strengths and limitations, he becomes watchful and alert to exercise self-control when needed. When a person knows his weaknesses, he can eradicate them by his knowledge of good traits within him. Also by leading a moderate life, one is less prone to the temptation of sense objects which leads to possession of self-control. When one refines his thoughts, he turns away from crude indulgence of senses.

An unattached attitude helps us to keep a check on our thoughts and actions. A person may outwardly control his actions and call himself a man of self-control. But this is not enough. True self-control means one does not feel the need to think of the sense objects. This happens when a person transforms himself and raises himself in his own eyes. By adopting self-control, one can acquire a number of other divine attributes such as renunciation, non-attachment, purity and dispassion.

Does one have to control the mind or the senses? When you fix your mind on a higher ideal, you get completely absorbed and you give little attention to other unnecessary thoughts that may enter your mind or which are already present there. Imagine yourself standing at a bus stop waiting for a particular bus. Other buses will also come and stop at your stand but you do not give any attention to them since your mind is fixed at your own bus. Similarly, when our mind is fixed on God, the highest ideal, other thoughts—particularly those concerning sense enjoyment—will not get supportive attention even if they enter our mind. Not only that, your stored up memories will also fade away since they do not get any space to stay there. This is the surest method of self-control because if you are dictated by your senses, you are a failure in spiritual field. Sri Sathya Sai Baba says that the joy in being the master of senses is far greater than being their slave. If you conquer yourself, there is no need to conquer others.

Charity

Indian way of life attaches a very special significance to charity or *dana*. It has always been considered a meritorious deed. Serving others is also an act of charity. We have seen that people set aside a portion of their wealth for construction of public utilities such as temples, wells and rest houses at places of pilgrimage. There are a large number of charitable homes which are serving the poor and trying to mitigate their suffering.

The *Bhagavad Gita* says that to give is a duty. It further says that acts of sacrifice (*yajna*), charity (*dana*) and austerity (*tapa*) should not be abandoned because such acts are the purifiers of the wise. *Dana* along with *tapa* and *yajna* are the foundations of Indian culture. It is said that charitable works done for others are really done for one's own good as charity benefits the giver more than the receiver. However, that charity is the best that is given as a matter of duty to a deserving person who does nothing in return. Charity is compared to a tree in an orchard that gives its fruit to passers-by without expectation of any return. Charity given with expectations of return is a 'self-full' (selfish) charity which does no good to the giver.

We generally associate charity with giving away some portion of our earnings to the needy. But charity also means giving love, knowledge, help or service to others as long as we look for no benefit in giving. Gyan dana or charity of knowledge is considered to be the best charity. This underscores that charity of quality is better than the charity of quantity. We are all capable of giving something to others, provided we understand giving to be a sacred act. Even if we have no money to give in charity, we can do a lot good to others with our thoughts and actions. Praying for those who are in need of some help is also an act of charity.

There is another angle from which we can understand the meaning of charity. The Isha Upanishad says that the universe is the glory of God which includes all the life that exists on earth. This implies that the wealth we possess is not really ours but belongs to God and we are its trustees. Therefore, we should utilize the wealth that we possess for His cause, that is to remove the suffering of the poor.

Doing good to others not only means giving something to them in physical form, but also helping them find their true nature. One question which is often asked is how can we solve the problems of others when our own problems are troubling us? Here we must realize that we are created to depend on each other. We have to live in the world as a family and we must help each other, irrespective of whether or not we have our own problems. Our problems should be considered as an opportunity for us to grow. When we do that, our own problems do not interfere with our acts of charity.

However, charity should be given in a right way. Charity has no value if the money given is earned by wrongful means. The *Valmiki Ramayana* states that charity should be given without humiliating the taker as such charity destroys the giver. It is also said that giving is superior to receiving since giving earns a friend. If we help others, others will help us unasked. Giving to others in whatever form teaches us to help the needy. People become great only when they realize that doing good to others is greater than helping our own self. All religions of the world give utmost importance to charity. Buddhism says that giving is a saving. The wise man will share whatever he has with others. Charity given anonymously is the best charity. *The Bible* says you should not make a big show of something that you give to a needy person and you must give it in such a way that even your closest friend does not know about it. Charity to the needy is one of the five pillars of Islam.

Swami Vivekananda said that if you get a chance to serve the needy, you should consider yourself to be a chosen one. You should bow before the taker for giving you the opportunity to serve him. Such is the significance of charity in the Indian way of life.

Renunciation

Renunciation (*Tyaga*) is a very common word which forms an inseparable part of the Vedantic or Hindu philosophy. Yet, the true meaning of *tyaga* is not well understood by many of us. Renunciation or *tyaga* is generally understood as physical *sanyasa* or renunciation of worldly life and retirement into forests for spiritual growth. Renunciation in its true sense has nothing to do with your physical location. One can be a *tyagi* while living in his home with family and one may not achieve the feeling of renunciation while living in forest all by oneself. If that be so, then how can we define true renunciation or *tyaga*?

Renunciation is an inner feeling that comes when one feels that he is the master of his inner life and he has given up evil thoughts, evil actions and evil way of life. Renunciation comes when one has abandoned all attachments and personal likes and dislikes and annihilated his ego. Renunciation is not of wealth but of the sense of possession of the wealth. Renunciation is also giving up of selfish desires. *Tyaga* is a feeling of living for the good of others.

Renunciation is in the heart of all religions. Hinduism accords a very high importance to renunciation. One of the six attributes of the Supreme Almighty or *Bhagvan* is renunciation. A man can never assume God-like disposition unless he is a *tyagi*. The real peace is found in a mind which has understood and practised *tyaga*. Renunciation helps to preserve energy within a person.

The *Bhagavad Gita* has given the real meaning of *tyaga*. It says that renunciation is not giving up something but catching up to a higher ideal. When you are established on a higher ideal, it automatically loosens your grip on lower impulses which finally fade away. Renunciation of fruit of action is one of the main tenets of the the *Bhagavad Gita*. In fact, it is a precondition to self-realization. It considers renunciation of the fruit of action far more superior to meditation as it results in peace. When a man is attached to the results of his actions, he becomes self-centred and restless and peace drifts away from him.

Renunciation of the fruit of action does not mean indifference to results. It only means no hankering after the results of your actions and concentrating fully on the work in hand. It means doing your allotted duties whole-heartedly, whatever may be the results. Since action cannot be totally relinquished by a human being in body form, those who renounce the fruit of action are real *tyagis*. Obligatory work in the form of sacrifice, gift and austerity should never be renounced or relinquished but should be performed giving up attachment, sense of doership and without caring for the fruit of action. The state of desire-free action about which the *Bhagavad Gita* talks is a great reward and this state can only be reached by acquiring a spirit of renunciation.

Renunciation is achieved not by escapism but by rightful involvement in all activities of life which are assigned to a man by virtue of his position or status in the society. Renunciation is reached by eradication of selfishness. It is gained by constructive reorganization of life. Renunciation follows when one decides to live as a part of the universe and not by living in isolation. The more we think in terms of doing good to others and the more we become impersonal (unselfish), the more we acquire the spirit of renunciation.

Renunciation does not imply giving up family but it is getting rid of desires and attachment even while staying with the family. Renunciation and Service are twin ideals of Indian thought of living that greatly help shape our personality in a positive way.

Peacefulness

Culture of peace is culture of life whereas culture of violence is culture of death. Peace is a state where the mind remains restful, unaffected by the happenings around. Peace can be termed the national religion of India. Peace is the essence of the *Vedas*. At the end of the Vedic prayers, there is chanting of peace, '*Om, Shanti, Shanti, Shanti*'. A popular Vedic prayer reads, 'May there be peace in heaven, sky, earth, water, plants and trees. May all be happy, May all be healthy, May all see auspiciousness, and May none suffer'. *Sarve santu niramaya* means may everyone be free from disease. Peace includes both inner and outer peace. Positively peace is social justice.

It is often said that name, fame, power and temptations do not give us permanent peace. It is true in the sense that such desires when fulfilled do not give contentment since we would long for more. When we get name and fame, we appear peaceful but this too is temporary. Real peace eludes us. If one performs good deeds, name and fame will come automatically to him, but one should not have any desire for it. If one establishes oneself in goodness, he will have perfect peace within himself and whatever name and fame he earns will not disturb his inner poise. Knowledge leads us to freedom—the more free we are, the more peaceful shall we become. Healthy and positive thoughts give us a peaceful disposition.

In spite of advances made by science and technology, religion still exercises a powerful influence. Religion is a source of peace since it raises our level of consciousness, expands our vision, dissolves our impurities, and takes us beyond dogmas and rituals.

Rabindranath Tagore said that peace can only come when our minds are filled with generosity and goodwill towards all. Love for all and hatred for none is bound to make us calm and peaceful. We have to remember that peace has an important role to play for our self-improvement as well as progress of mankind.

Peace is essential for the survival of civilization. Good governance can remove conflicts within the society and lead the countrymen to the ultimate state of peacefulness. The basic unit of peace has to be cultivated at the level of individual personality.

Real peace is an end product which has no rival, no alternative. One can understand the real meaning of peace only when one is at peace with oneself—a state of freedom from disturbance, agitation, violence and anxiety. Peace comes when one removes negative instincts and fills up himself with truth, non-violence, love and righteousness. Martin Luther King said that true peace is not merely an absence of tension; it is the presence of justice and brotherhood. Only a peaceful person can live in harmony with others and natural environment. If you become peaceful yourself, the world will become peaceful by one more person. If we accept that others have an equal right to peace, then we have a responsibility to make others peaceful. The *Bhagavad Gita* gives an unfailing method of attaining peace. It says give up future of your action, peace will automatically descend on you.

Study of Scriptures

In the *Bhagavad Gita*, Lord Krishna tells warrior Arjun, "Let scriptures be your authority in ascertaining what ought to be done and what ought not to be done." This brings us the necessity of studying scriptures in order to understand our duties in the world. Study of scripture like the *Bhagavad Gita* brings in positive vibrations and thought current in mind. One who studies scriptures constantly dwells on noble thoughts. By studying scriptures, we convert our knowledge into wisdom. Gandhiji said that it is the duty of every cultured men and women to read sympathetically the scriptures of the world. Study of scriptures is highlighted in our *Upanishads*. After students complete their studies and get set to step out of *Brahamcharya Ashram*, the teacher tells them that one should not neglect the study of scriptures. It is as good as our prayers which increase our faith in God, besides removing our negativity and disappointments. It provides necessary inspiration to us to live a divine life while performing our day to day work. Study of scriptures, whose Sanskrit equivalent is *swadhyaya,* also means self-study, self-introspection, self-evaluation, self-awareness, self-criticism, self-judging, self-selection and self-rejection. We should set aside some time every day from our routine for scriptural study to increase our strength and remove our weaknesses.

The study of scriptures must be followed by reflecting on their teachings and to get purified from within. Knowledge acquired from the study of scriptures and aided by reflection and reason provides us with an eye of wisdom. One can transform his worldly nature into spiritual nature by the study of scriptures. To understand God's will and to act on it, it is necessary that we live according to the dictates of scriptures. The study of scriptures evolves one's thought processes and gives clarity in thinking.

Other divine attributes which need to be understood and practised are tolerance, absence of anger, compassion, humility and a spirit of sacrifice.

Tolerance means accepting and respecting others' viewpoints. It means accepting others in totality, giving space to others and accommodating others in your scheme of things. All this leads to mutual respect for each other. Exercising tolerance is all the more required in a country like India which has a diverse society. People staying here belong to different religions and castes and might face conflict of interests. English philosopher CEM Joad held that tolerance means accepting the viewpoints of others even when you think that they are wrong.

Absence of anger is another divine trait that can do wonders to our personality. It means not losing your poise when confronted with annoying people and unfavourable situations. It is in one's capacity to check wave of anger at the right time so that it does not manifest in our actions. You may have a tendency to wear anger sometimes to tell people that you are angry and annoyed with them so that they improve upon their behaviour. When you wear anger, people do as you want them to do even when you are really not angry at the core. Anger is described in the *Bhagavad Gita* as one of the three gates to hell; the other two being desire and greed. To control anger is a must for a balanced personality. Those who go wild in anger realize when they are calm that it was not worth the pain. Psychologists have often suggested delayed reaction as an antidote against anger.

Compassion can be discovered through love alone. It does not mean taking pity on others. Compassion for others arises when we accept others' pain as our own. It sweetens life. Dalai Lama says, "It is the enemy who can truly teach us to practise the virtues of compassion and tolerance." Humility is the characteristic of greatness. It comes with knowledge and wisdom. The more knowledgeable a person becomes, the more humility he acquires. Humility brings stability. Low-lying areas receive water from all sides. Everything will come running where there is humility. It is said that as pride comes before fall, humility comes before rise. I will add here that humility stays with the person even after he has risen in the same manner as a tree laden with fruits is bent. The spirit of sacrifice means working for the good of others.

The ultimate aim of practising divine virtues is to attain purity of mind. Purity is the intermediary between Man and God. Blessed are those who are pure as they will see God, says Jesus in *The Sermon on The Mount*. It is the impure mind that hides the divine spark within and does not allow it to manifest in our thoughts, speech and actions. So, we have to cleanse the mind to ultimately get rid of our selfish and non-divine traits. But how do we move from selfishness to selflessness? This needs to be thoroughly studied.

From Selfishness to Selflessness

Selfishness is the basis of all immoral and corrupt practices that are prevalent in our society. Our worldly desires make us self-centred and to fulfil them we focus on self-interest and become selfish. The main cause of selfishness is that we only think about our own interests and comforts. Selfishness starts fading into the background once we start thinking about others, their problems and what we can do to reduce them. Selfishness is the biggest impurity in us which does not permit us to look beyond our own self. Once we are rooted in selfishness, we move away from truth and at the same time show very little true respect for others and their opinion. Swami Vivekananda remarked that what is selfish is immoral and what is unselfish is moral. People are selfish due to a wrong understanding that if their desires are met, they can be happy forever. They fail to realize that the main purpose of life is not the pursuit of material happiness. It is the pursuit of eternal happiness which has nothing to do with material happiness. It is obtained by looking inward to realize our spiritual destiny. The world is tempting and eye-catching and gives instant joy to a worldly man. But desires can never be satiated by gratifications. The more they are enjoyed, the more they grow as fire grows by the pouring of butter into it.

Man performs three types of actions which can be put under three heads—selfish actions, unselfish actions and selfless actions. Selfish actions are those which are based on your needs and also on your greed. These actions are performed to cater to selfish desires. Unselfish actions might be based on selfish desires but behind them is some sort of unselfish goal like contribution towards betterment of society. Then there are selfless actions which are not propelled by any desires but by a sense of duty towards the betterment of surroundings or environment. For a selfless man everything other than himself is environment; not only the trees, rivers or plants but also all living being around him. Selfless actions are basically duty-driven actions where man considers it his duty to act for others and even goes out of the way to help others; particularity those who are in need. Selfless work is the highest type of work and selfless people are assets to society. They are those who set example for the ordinary people. Selfless persons do not expect any reward for their actions.

The *Bhagavad Gita* defines Yoga as skill in action or efficiency in action. We perform skillful actions and give our one hundred per cent when we do not have personal interest in the work. Man's selfishness leads to inefficiency. Corruption, poverty, crime, violence and backwardness in society are all caused by inefficiency in work. Efficient work is performed where there is sincerity, commitment, transparency and rightful attitude.

So what is the way out of selfishness? Swami Vivekananda said that selflessness is life, selfishness is death. When we act as per the sense of duty, we are not victim of (our impulses). To wake up to the world of spirit, we have to fight selfishness. Man's aim in life is not eating for himself or working for his personal needs. Man lives in a community which can run only on exchange of commodities and services. The *Bhagavad Gita* admonishes those who are selfish and says that those who cook for their own sake and do not share with other are thieves. It is very appropriately said that one who is content to go alone will never go to heaven. This brings us to a very noble idea that we should share with others which is the hallmark of Indian culture. We have to bring about a change in our attitude towards life. We should move from an attitude of hoarding to the attitude of sharing. Share your knowledge with others and it would increase manyfold.

Giving is important to root out selfishness. Give preference to giving rather than taking from others. The joy of giving is several times more than the joy of taking from others. To root out selfishness, one should involve oneself with charitable acts. Another way to shun selfishness is to replace self-interest by social interest. You should undertake social work with a sense of responsibility and with a conviction to change the society for better. One should make selfless service to others as the basic aim of one's social work. The answer to the question why should one serve others is very simple. A man benefits himself by doing good to others. When a man establishes himself in benevolence, his selfish thoughts decline and he moves onto the path of enlightenment. He acquires wisdom which is higher than intellectuality. A wise person is always selfless whereas an intellectual can be selfish. And finally, when you inject 'duty idea' into your life, you shall ever remain selfless.

One thing was common in all great people of the world: they were selfless workers. Selflessness comes from the cessation of desires. Desire means a feeling of deficiency. Desires are not to be suppressed but controlled with inner blossoming. You may draw enjoyment when associated with beautiful things but you should never develop attachment and craving for them. The moment the world becomes unselfish, evil will disappear. When you root out selfishness from within, inner self will blossom.

To develop our personality, we need to be 'a person of values'. The values that make our life meaningful are referred to as higher values of life. For example, dharma or righteousness is a unique Indian value which separates human beings from animals. Dharma guides a man to regulate his wealth and desire within the parameter of righteousness and work out his liberation or salvation from the cycle of birth and death. A valueless person lives without any purpose. He does not live but just exists. We can pick up higher values of life at any point of time irrespective of one's age, but the best time to learn them is when we are young. When values are introduced in our education system, we shall be inclined towards personality development from young age.

The *gurukul* system of education which India had adopted was discontinued during the British rule. The reasons why the British discontinued this system were given by Lord Macaulay in the British Parliament in February 1835. The extract from his speech runs as follows:

"I have travelled across the length and breadth of India and I have not seen one person who is a beggar, or who is a thief. Such wealth I have seen in this country, such high moral values, people of such calibre that I do not think we would ever conquer this country unless we break the very backbone of this nation which is her spiritual and cultural heritage. And therefore, I propose that we replace her old and ancient education system; her culture. If the Indians think that all that is foreign and English is good and greater than their own they will lose their self-esteem, their native self-culture and they will become what we want them, a truly dominated nation."

Lord Macaulay conspired against us. The education system that we are following in India today is actually the

British education system, which is inclined towards science and materialism. Science cannot provide foundation to values. It gradually eliminates values and metaphysical concept. Value education is a matter of widespread social concern.

Introduce Values in Education

In ancient days, India followed the *gurukul* system of education where students were placed under direct supervision of a teacher. Indian sacred literature like the *Vedas* and the *Upanishads* formed the core of teaching in these *gurukuls*. In this educational system, a number of subjects were taught including Mathematics, Astronomy, Astrology, Ethics, Agriculture, Poetry, Dance, Art, Dharma, Medicine and Surgery. Education imparted to the students was holistic in nature since it looked after all segments of student's personality—physical, mental, intellectual, emotional and, most importantly, spiritual. In the *Chandogya Upanishad*, it is stated that how valueless is all learning unless education includes knowledge of self or spirit. It also says that knowledge of self is the highest knowledge—*Adhyatma vidya vidyanam*. In ancient India, emphasis was laid to teach basic Indian values drawn from our scriptures—values such as truth, honesty, oneness of all existence, equality, purity of mind, tolerance, dharma or righteousness, love, peace, forgiveness, service, non-violence and selflessness. Social values like obedience, friendliness, cooperativeness, compassion and self-discipline were also included in our education system. The education aimed at building the character of students on the solid foundation of righteousness.

Present-day education imparted to students in India is not directed towards wholesome building of student's character and personality. Moral, ethical and spiritual values are not included comprehensively in what is being taught. It mainly focusses on cultivation of academic knowledge that provides skill to the students to secure suitable jobs. Also, in today's educational system, the spiritual element, which is the greatest asset of India, is missing altogether—the education is examination and degree oriented. It is for this reason that people coming out of educational institutions are lacking in wisdom and moral courage even when they are well qualified. While on the one side of society we see wealth and comfort, on the other side there is violence and hatred. Our present education system is devoid of value orientation and it does not help in character building of the students.

The Indian thought on education is that education is not indoctrination. India always considered education as medium of transmission of its spiritual heritage, culture and civilization. All civilizations have been built on the foundation of a certain system of education. The Indian concept of education aimed at enriching one's life so that the man became a good human being displaying appropriate qualities at secular and spiritual levels. The usefulness of Indian literature is acknowledged by German Indologist Max Muller who said that it is Indian literature which can make our life perfect, comprehensive and universal.

While we may not be able to revive the *gurukul* system of education, we must ensure that the fundamental principles underlying the ancient Indian educational system are preserved, adopted and re-expressed in modern thought. Our education system has to be value based as per the Indian religious, spiritual, and cultural ethos. Globalization and consumerism based on the progress of science and technology have made us materialistic in our outlook due to which we tend to ignore the real meaning of education in the Indian context. It is true that educational qualifications are required for seeking jobs in the competitive world of today, but it should not mean that education is just an instrument of securing jobs for the students. We have to take education beyond jobs. There is a definite conflict between progress of science and its applications and value-based education. Therefore, we have to adopt a balance between scientific advancements and Indian values of life in our education, ensuring that value-based education occupies an honoured place in our teaching system. This requires an attitudinal change in the minds of all those who are directly involved with our educational system. More than 100 years ago, Swami Vivekananda said that education imparted to our students should not only be academic but should cater to life building, man making and character building. He appreciated the western values like scientific temper, rational investigation, work efficiency and teamwork and wanted these to be combined with the Indian values which entirely focussed on character building of students. In addition to teaching moral and spiritual values, students should also be exposed to the discipline of arts and science. Art discipline includes drawing, painting, photography, sculpture, music, dance and drama. Art experience spreads love, peace, compassion, expands human consciousness and awakes vital energy from within. Participation in art discipline is a creative activity. Education should also aim to sensitize students to curb rudeness and make them aware of the importance of refined behaviour. Only that education which would be holistic in nature could meet the requirement to build all elements of a student's personality.

Indian culture is deep rooted in spirituality and it would be tragic if India throws away her spiritual heritage and does not include it in its education. Spirituality is based on the foundation of morality and morality draws its strength from religion. Therefore, we cannot turn away from religion on the plea that we are a secular state, since morality and religion are closely connected. We have to devise a method through which religious and moral teachings of all major religions are harmoniously integrated in our education system. It would not be out of place to mention that our national policy on education formed in 1986 mentioned inclusion of moral, ethical, social and spiritual values from all religions in the teaching curriculum.

In a pluralistic society of India, children need more valuè-oriented education to experience unity among diverse traditions. Moral degeneration found in our society can only be checked by imparting moral and spiritual values which should be a part of our education system. Without religion, there can be no morality and without a moral base spiritual outlook cannot be developed.

Swami Vivekananda defined education as manifestation of potential divinity within the child. Since the divinity is same in all, its comprehension gives the idea of oneness of all existence. Students should be made to realize this by inculcating moral and higher values of life in them. Once the sense of equality enters the mind of our students, there shall be a gradual decline in base inclinations like hatred, violence and jealously, and higher values of life like love, peace, compassion and brotherhood would prosper. This is how a spiritual outlook can be developed among students. Spiritual outlook also improves the performance of students as they work without any personal motive in a spirit of serving others. To achieve a spiritual outlook among students, which is the most essential in the present time, moral and higher values of life should be included in our education system. It is also to be emphasized that for an overall personality development of a student, moral and spiritual empowerment is as important as economic empowerment.

While literacy is the starting point of education, the ultimate end of education is building character. To achieve that, value system cannot be separated from religion. Value education to be effective needs to be integrated into the regular teaching subjects and should not be made one subject unrelated to the rest. There is no use of training one teacher in moral values. All teachers should be fully capable of teaching moral values to the students. In fact, value system should permeate to the entire organization. Heads of the institutions should become the path setters to spread values among students. We also need to think in terms of forming an advisory body to monitor the spread of value-based education in our education system. The advisory body should consist of enlightened citizens and educational thinkers, who should also advise the educational institutes on ways and means to teach higher values of life to the students. Value education aids like prayers, meditation and yoga; debates and essay competitions on value education; activities like celebration of inter-faith festivals should be made use of to impart value education.

It is high time we give a practical shape to value education to make our students realize its value in shaping their character. Educational institutes are agencies where values of life can be inculcated and internalized. With the cultivation of values, individual knowledge will turn into wisdom and people of wisdom will be valued in the society. Values remove narrow-mindedness and make our youth think big and act big with a spiritual outlook. Twenty-first Century is the age of transition where a feeling of insecurity and restlessness exists due to widespread violence, hatred and fundamentalism. We need values now more than any other time for providing a direction to our youth as well as our elders to live in the world with morality. Elimination of poverty, ignorance, ill health, casteism can only be made possible if we become morally upright.

We should never consider that we are born ordinary. We may be born ordinary but we should not end our life as an ordinary person. The key to personality development is to go after our goal with full vigour. Author Paulo Coelho says that if we go after to achieve something with full throttle or in totality, the whole universe sides with us to reach our goal. According to Helen Keller, we can do anything we want if we stick to it long enough. We have to be constant in our effort.

Constancy is a Virtue

The dictionary defines constancy as firmness, endurance and faithfulness. It is steadfastness in whatever we do. Constancy is a positive sign and if one clings to it in the process of self-elevation, one is bound to succeed. Very often we get highly influenced by someone's good quality or by what we read but we do not dwell upon it constantly. Due to this, we allow a chance of bettering ourselves slip out of our hands. While it is important that we keep the door and windows of our mind open to catch something good, it is more important to stick to the goodness we have caught. Then only goodness becomes a part of us. As we are constantly aware of our home, our family and friends without making any effort for doing so, in the same way we should also be constantly aware of some good qualities which we may have come across, so that we acquire them permanently. In fact, constant awareness of our strength helps us to rebuild ourselves. Similarly, we also have to be constantly aware of our negativity so that we throw it out symbolically.

The virtues discussed above have to be imbibed by continuous practice. Purity of mind has to precede spirituality. Just as coloured water penetrates a white cloth freely, the teachings of scriptures enter quickly in a pure mind. There are no shortcuts in becoming morally upright. One has to traverse every inch of ground to become a righteous person, setting an example for others to follow him. Mark Twain beautifully said that less a man knows bigger the noise he makes. One who boasts does not know and one who knows does not talk about it unless asked. Great personalities of India were invariably morally sound and upright.

> Morality is not the doctrine of how we may make ourselves happy, but how we may make ourselves worthy of happiness.
>
> ***Immanuel Kant***

Some Traits of Positive Personality

There is nothing so disobedient as an undisciplined mind, and there is nothing so obedient as a disciplined mind.

Gautam Buddha

Core of any religious philosophy is to understand the purpose of life. It is essential, therefore, to understand what human life is all about. One way of looking at life is that a man enters the world from one door and leaves it from another. He enters the world when he is born; he grows up, gets educated, obtains a job for his living, gets married, brings up children, gets old, and leaves the world by another door at the end of his life span. Is this a correct way to describe human life? Those who believe in this life-chain, live mechanically from birth to death. But life is more than a mechanical existence. Life provides plenty of adventures and opportunities to those who live every moment of it mindfully. So, what exactly is life? We have a few options to describe human life as perceived by our men of wisdom.

Life is Yoga

Our great spiritual philosopher Sri Aurobindo said that all life is Yoga. Yoga is defined as the method of connecting individual soul to the Supreme Soul. This concept is based on the Hindu ideology that human life should be utilized to make an honest attempt to realize God.

The soul inside a man is potentially divine and while living in the world we should direct our entire effort to unite the individual soul with the supreme soul and to free ourselves from the cycle of birth and death. 'All life is Yoga' implies that whatever we do in life is done in a spirit of dedication towards God. It never means that we should discard the world and live in a forest to realize God. It only means that we should live in world and do our best to contribute towards world solidarity with our mind settled in God-consciousness. This is in conformity with the *Bhagavad Gita* that says, "Remember Me at all times and fight… Conduct yourself in the world while firmly established in God."

Life is a School

Sri Aurobindo further said that life is a school where learning process never ends. In this process of learning, earth is considered as a big classroom. When we accept that life is a school, we accept that life teaches us if we keep our minds open. The *Rig Veda* says that let noble thoughts enter our mind from all sides. We can learn from anyone, even from those who are younger to us in age. In the *Bhagavatam*, Sage Dattatreya said that if we keep our eyes and ears open we will find that everything that exists in nature around us, even birds and animals, have a lesson to teach us. Dattatreya talks about 24 gurus from whom he had learnt. For example, the earth teaches forbearance and tree is an excellent example of selfless service since it provides shade to all without any expectation of return. But why should we learn throughout our life? It is because learning makes us gain both worldly and spiritual wisdom. Learning enables us to unlearn or weed out what is unwanted or undesirable in our mind. Learning enables us to find newer interests in life: it gives us freedom, makes us observe the reality, and, at the same time, enlightens us to change our perceptions. Therefore, be not a scholar but a brilliant student. Develop sun-like affection, river-like generosity and earth-like hospitality.

Life is a Battlefield

Dr Radhakrishnan said that life is a battle between spirit and matter, knowledge and ignorance, self-control and temptation, and between discrimination and sensual life. When we commence to fight this battle, then begins our journey from human life to divine life. Life is a battle because no one will give room to you; you will have to create one for yourself. Human life is not programmed. We have a free will to be what we want. When we look inwardly, we find that we are fighting the inner battle continuously. Fighting the outer battle of life means tackling our day-to-day problems related to ourselves, our family, our profession and our society. Since man lives in two world, outer and inner, he has to simultaneously fight these battles. This is needed for his evolution and for him to become a useful member of the society. The hardest battle you have to fight is the battle to be just you shorn of the embellishments.

Life is a Train Journey

Life can also be compared to a train journey where we all are travelling towards our destination. We meet new people who enter our compartment and then there are those who leave us never to meet again. In worldly life, we meet some people for the first time and lose some forever. Our relationships in life are not permanent as people come and go on a regular basis. While some people come into our life and quickly go away, some stay for a while and leave footprints in our hearts. Sometimes the train passes through green fields, sometimes it passes through a barren ground and sometimes it passes through a tunnel. This compares to the pleasant and unpleasant situations which we come across in life. There are some in the train who are travelling in higher class while the majority is in lower class. In the journey of life, those who are travelling in higher class are the ones who are spiritually evolved. Their number is very small as compared to the worldly people who are travelling in lower class.

Life is a Celebration

Sri Sri Ravi Shankar, a spiritual teacher and humanitarian par excellence and founder of the Art of Living Foundation, calls life a celebration. He himself is cheerfulness personified. He says that man has become too serious in life and forgets to smile. He asks human beings to smile and serve, to meditate, and to celebrate. Sri Sri Ravi Shankar says that if the sun rises and celebrates, rivers flow and celebrate, and trees flower and celebrate, why cannot human beings evolve and celebrate life. Spirituality is not seriousness but cheerfulness. Life can be joyful if we learn to celebrate even the smallest moment and event. Consider each day as the best day of your life.

So what is human life all about and what should we do in life? The answer is simple. We should become a *yogi* and learn from every moment of life. We should fight the battle of life to undertake the journey from human life to divine life. We should celebrate life as we celebrate any festival because life is a beautiful experience. While doing so, we should remember Lord Krishna's advice to Arjuna in the *Bhagavad Gita* that we should live life in a spirit of *yajna* or sacrifice doing our best to look after the welfare of others. Do not cook food only for yourself because if you do that then you are a thief. Life is not to be measured in months or years but by inner completion and happiness. We understand the value of life, the beauty of life and all what life gives us when we realize the pointlessness and irrelevance of living an ordinary life. Life is as much about achieving as it is about contributing. Life is to be lived purposefully which means that one should live in the present. Living in the present means living with mindfulness so that irrelevant thoughts do not occupy space in our mind.

Mindfulness has been described in Buddhism as a calm awareness of one's body functions, feelings, content of consciousness, or consciousness itself. Most important thing is that mindfulness keeps you under control and does not allow you to go astray. Mindfulness practice is increasingly being employed in the western psychology to alleviate a variety of mental and physical conditions including obsessive-compulsive disorder, anxiety and treatment of depression and drug addiction. Most important thing is it helps control time by making one completely immersed in an act.

Our purpose of existence is not just to go with the flow of life but to understand as to why we are here. To understand the purpose of life we have to find out the answers to the questions —Who Am I? Where have I come from? What is my purpose of coming to the world? And where do I go after leaving the world? Am I the body which grows and decays or am I the soul inside the body which never dies being indestructible? Spiritual life begins with this basic question and as it progresses, it also provides the answer to these questions. Ramana Maharishi, one of the greatest saints of our country has based his teachings on the answer to the question, Who Am I? According to Ramana Maharishi, enquiring persistently about this question leads us to answers of the same. As the thought of 'I' vanishes, leaving the Supreme Non-dual Soul alone, our false identification with our body vanishes and we realize that in essence we are not the body but the soul. 'I Am *Brahman*' is one of the *mahavakya* (great truth) of Hindu philosophy.

Gautam Buddha started his search for truth after seeing old men and the dead. If all who are born must decay and die, the purpose of life cannot be to just pass life the way it comes. The purpose of life must be to find answers to existence and elevating one's life through knowledge and enlightenment. Buddha left everything for this search of truth.

While we have come to the world to realize our spiritual identity (the soul, *atma* or the spark of the Supreme) within us, we also have to participate in the material life. So our aim of coming to the world becomes twofold: to uplift ourselves with a view to identify with the Supreme Spirit and to contribute towards making the world a better place to live. Each man is born with a purpose to do something in the world and when we raise our level of consciousness, our purpose of life becomes clearer with each day. It is our duty to accept life as it is and find out the purpose of our living, and achieve our aim.

Man is not born in this world by his own choice. Also, a man does not come out suddenly out of nothing. The theory of rebirth propounded by the *Vedanta* or Hindu Philosophy gives answer to the question of birth and death. The karma theory of rebirth says that man takes birth as per the effect of the karma of his past lives. Not only man takes birth as per the effect of his past deeds, he also faces pleasures and pains depending upon the quality of deeds done in past lives. If his past deeds have been good, he would face happiness in the life and if his past deeds have been bad, he would experience pain. This is the karmic theory or the theory of cause and effect in life and death. That is the reason why some of us are born rich, some poor, some with certain characteristic and the others without any specific traits. Some experience happiness in life while others sorrow.

William Shakespeare described the world as a stage where people comes with a pre-determined script, plays his or her part and departs at a pre-defined time. That may be a comparison but there is a big difference between the two. The stage artist is given the entire script of the play and he knows his part in the drama till the end. But this does not happen in human life as a man does not know his future since he is not handed over the entire script of the life before he begins to act in it. This in my view is a blessing. Imagine how boring life would be if a man knew in advance what is in store for him. Man has a free will to decide whether to act or not to act in a given situation, whereas stage artist participating in a drama does not have the choice to deviate from a written script.

There are some traits which a person with a positive personality ought to possess. He should believe that he can work out his destiny with his work. He knows the cause of his sufferings and also the reason for not achieving the best. Next, a person with a positive personality should have a positive attitude. He should have self-esteem, he should love to serve others, and he must have the ability to learn from life as it unfolds itself. He should have a detached disposition, he should have faith in God, he should feel that he has the freedom to act and is not driven by life and, last but not the least, he should think of complementing others rather than competing with them.

Is Fate Unalterable or Negotiable?

When we talk about free will we have to understand as to what extent we are free and what is the relationship between free will and fate. Are free will and fate opposed to each other or are they expressions of one and the same thing? Or, if there is fate, is it outside man's control? The conflict between the doctrine of human freedom and predestination always attracted intense debate.

When things do not happen in life the way we want them to be, there is a temptation to attribute our failure to fate or destiny. This helps derive some consolation. Fate does play a part in man's life but there is also a free will which a man possesses and which enables him to take his work to its highest state of efficiency. Hence, we can assume that both free will and fate regulate our life.

Free will and fate can be called the two legs men walk on. They can also be referred to as two wheels of a cart where both play their part in its movement. A man is caught between his free will and fate and it would be fatal not to recognize one or the other. Free will is the exercising of will while performing actions in the present life, whereas fate is the sum total of the effects of actions of our previous lives which influence our present life. When a cause produces an effect, we call it fate. Fate, which is also called *prarabdha*, is that portion of our past actions which is bearing fruit in our present life. The law of karma states that each one of us is an effect of which our past has been the cause. Our past actions can be good as well as bad which produce corresponding effect in our present life. In broader sense, we can say that free will and fate are one and the same thing as both are grounded on exercise of free will—one in the present life and the other in our past lives. Though we have a free will but freedom to choose rightly depends upon our moral training. Wrong use of force will result in violence and substandard acts.

Even though fate or destiny plays some part in our present life, human life is not mathematically predestined. Human beings are endowed with free will and it should be employed righteously and purposefully for our self-evolution. That we have a free will is endorsed by a single verse in the *Bhagavad Gita*. At the end of His discourse, Lord Krishna tells Arjuna to reflect on what He has said and act as he likes. If everything in life was predestined then God would not have told Arjuna to act as he thinks what is right. Fate or destiny is usually described by an average mind as whatever has to happen will happen and man can do nothing to change the course of events which are destined for him as fate. This thinking is not rational. This thinking makes us feel that we are just puppets in the hands of God waiting for something to happen. But when we evolve ourselves, we find that we are not just puppets but we are partners of God in cosmic activities. Albert Einstein said we are co-creators with God and not puppets. We have seen that in life people do take up challenges and fight their way out to obtain favourable results. Once we accept that everything in life is dictated by fate, we close all doors to our progress. We also adopt the path of the least resistance and wait for things to happen rather than making things happen. It is very rightly said that if one door closes for us then other doors open. But as human beings we have a tendency to look at the closed door for a long period instead of looking and exploring the possibility to make use of the doors which have been opened. The best is to treat the obstacles created by fate as an opportunity to put in sustained effort to get over them. Obstacles created by fate should be recognized, dealt with, and defeated by the power of our efforts. Self-effort precedes God's grace which goes well with the adage that God helps those who help themselves.

Those who are inclined to believe in free will are always gainers as they are prepared to act and not give up. When Winston Churchill was asked to give one reason for his success against heavy odds, he said, "Do Not, Do Not, Do Not, Do Not, Do Not give up." The ill effects of the sins of the past do not dishearten those who believe in free will as they act positively to neutralize them. They know that self-effort and good deeds of their present life shall dilute the ill effects of their past deeds, as milk poured in black tea soothes its blackness. Sri Aurobindo said that we are our fate through our actions. Other saints and sages have always relied on the self-effort in present life to create a man's fate. Lord Krishna says in the *Bhagavad Gita* that a man should stand up and fight; meaning exertion and not submission to fate. Sage Vashishta while instructing Lord Rama said that fate or the effects of our past deeds is like a child and our effort of the present life is like a youth. And in the fight between youth and child, youth shall always be the winner. This conveys that fate loses its bite when confronted with self-effort. In the *Mahabharata*, Bhishma conveyed the same idea when he said that exertion is greater than destiny and action shapes destiny and not the other way round. That is why wise people do not rely on fate but focus on self-effort. God has planned our whole life before we are born but He has not planned our day-to-day actions and our precise words and thoughts which are controlled by us.

At an average state of consciousness, man should not set his mind on fate otherwise he would lose interest in life. As our level of consciousness improves we realize the part played by fate or the unknown hand in our life. Interconnectedness between free will and fate is explained in the *Bhagavad Gita* which states that there are five causes for the accomplishment of all work. Out of these, four causes—the seat of action, the agent, various senses and manifold efforts—are under human control. The fifth cause which is called unseen force or past karma, fate or *daivam* (presiding divinity) is outside man's control. The non-human factor's share in our action is sometimes evident when despite best efforts we do not obtain desired results for our actions. Here, a man should not get disappointed because all powers rest on absolute justice. If anything appears unjust it would mean that the process of divine justice has not yet finished. Belief in the *daivam* or the fifth cause should not become an excuse for lack of self-effort. The fifth cause ensures that a man cannot become author of results of action which he undertakes. When Lord Krishna showed his divine form to Arjuna, he told him that all warriors standing against him have been doomed to die under divine dispensation. Even without Arjuna, they shall not live since they have already been killed by Him. Arjuna is just an instrument or merely an occasion in the divine plan and he should conquer the enemy in the battle. This certainly does not mean that God has predestined this event but it only reinforces cause and effect syndrome due to which the warriors have to meet their end as an effect of their past deed. God sees far ahead and all moments of time—past, present and future exist in the same time frame for divine spirit. Everything is permitted by God and he knows the goal of all lives.

Can the effect of bad karmas be totally obliterated? When a man surrenders to God, renounces the fruits of his actions and offers them to God then fate does not affect him. When man rises towards perfection, his free will merges with the divine will. Then God works through him as he has surrendered before Him. Ramana Maharishi provided an apt answer when he said, "What would fate do if you have surrendered to God?" This is an appropriate concept which a man should adopt. There is always an advantage to accept that a man's fate is variable and not fixed. Though people think that fate is fixed, those who are enlightened accept that fate is negotiable and a man can shape his destiny with self-effort and surrender. When we confront an obstacle, we do not look at the opportunities available to us to negotiate the obstacle. Generally when one door closes, other doors open up but we have an in-built tendency to look only at the closed door only. Those who negotiate their fate do not look at the closed door for long. They always find a way out. Things may not always turn out to be favourable even for those who rely on self-effort. This is because a man has also to face some sufferings in the present life due to his past deeds.

Human Suffering

Two things disturb man considerably. One is when he undergoes suffering either physically or mentally, and two when he finds that he does not get recognition for his efforts. In both cases he compares himself with others who are considered to be better and draws his own conclusions. When a man suffers, he invariably asks—Why me? Then when he is not rewarded for his efforts his immediate reaction is 'Why not me?' He considers himself as good and at times even better than those whose efforts have won them recognition. Man is caught in the whirlpool of why me? and why not me? and continue to suffer unnecessarily.

Take the first case when a man undergoes sufferings in life. Man suffers not because of others' faults but due to his own misdoings in this life or in the lives past. The law of cause and effect or the law of karma underscores that man's actions would produce consequences as per their nature. Each individual is a separate entity as far as his worldly life is concerned though spiritually we all are one, as the same God permeates our soul. When a man is born on earth, the consequences of his past acts unfold in the present life giving joy and sorrow or pleasure and pain. When something goes wrong in our life, we are quick in putting the blame on others for our miseries. This is not a correct action. Man must accept responsibility of all happenings in his life since these are related to his own doings. He is himself responsible for all that is happening in his present life or should we say he is accountable for his acts of the past which are producing their effects in the present.

We can surely take action to mitigate our sufferings by performing good deeds which would reduce the effect of our suffering. The other thing which we should keep in mind is that the sufferings will also disappear as they are not meant to stay with us for the rest of our life. The best way of facing sufferings is rising above both pleasure and pain. When we transcend something, we do not involve ourselves in it. If you do not feel excited about pleasure of life then you would not be unduly disturbed by the pain you meet.

When man is not rewarded for his efforts, he becomes jealous of those who have obtained recognition. Jealousy produces hatred for others which, according to latest scientific data, is the root cause of diseases afflicting human body. If your efforts are not recognized or have not been awarded, you need to put in more efforts to achieve recognition. It is as simple and straightforward as that. If you believe in this you are bound to succeed. A sincere effort can never go waste. Everything happens at the right time. The moment you deserve, you would get what you deserve. The *Bhagavad Gita* advises us that man should work to the best of his ability and not bother himself with the results. If the result is favourable, your effort is acknowledged. If it is not then your effort is not up to the mark and you need to put in more; you must base your success on sincere hard work and not fluke. There is no need for consulting an astrologer if you believe that your hard work and sincerity shall always be acknowledged. Some failures do not mean that you lose interest in life. Have a zest for life and always give your best wholeheartedly. Always be energetic, genuine and honest and never pretend something which you actually are not. Always be yourself and use your free will to improve your performance.

We must also know our weaknesses and try to annihilate them by the process of self-analysis and self-examination. Make use of self-help. The *Bhagavad Gita* informs us that the man is his friend as well as enemy. It is your inner self which would always tell you whether you are good or bad. So hear your inner voice and act on it for self-elevation. When you act rightly based on your self-assessment, you are your best friend. If you act wrongly you are your own enemy. We must also remember that a man has an intuition higher than his intellect which can guide him to move in the right direction.

One should strive to be a man of values in addition to being a man of success. We have to build up certain qualities that define character. They are love, truthfulness, non-violence, righteousness and caring, sharing and accepting others. When we focus on such qualities, we develop ourselves internally and our life becomes active and dynamic both mentally as well as physically.

One thing that prevents us from developing a positive personality is that we lack a positive outlook in life. When we meet a person for the first time, his or her negative traits attract us more than the positive ones. When we have a positive approach, we will catch positive traits of others. The fault lies in us because we lack a positive attitude which makes us incomplete. A positive personality must develop a positive attitude which helps us to enrich life.

Positive Attitude Enriches Life

Our life is shaped by our thoughts. Man is essentially what his thoughts are. If we think positively our attitude towards life would become positive. But when we have a negative outlook, our life would become a bundle of negation. A person who thinks positive sends out positive thoughts around which activates his environment and he also draws back positive vibrations. The law of attraction says what we broadcast into environment, we get more of it. If we give vibrations of love through our thoughts, words and deeds, we would get more of love. Positive attitude helps us evolve inside and everything else becomes secondary. A positive person finds acceptance everywhere. On the other hand, our negative thoughts often make us dwell on the unpleasant past moments of our life. Our aim should be to remove negativity from our life. Negative thoughts containing anger, fear, self, ego, doubts, regrets and sadness. These drain away our energy and make us lazy. One should live in present without thinking of the past and without worrying for the future. When we invest in the present, we look after our future as well. We can follow certain guidelines which can assist us in removing negativity from our mind and help us to stay in a positive state:

No Fault Finding

When we try to find faults in others we lower ourselves and encourage the evil of others to enter our mind. Our scriptures tell us that there is no sin as grievous as counting faults of others. They are themselves faulty who try to locate faults in others. We should find our own faults and make a whole-hearted effort to set them right.

No Comparison with Others

Life is meant not to compete but complement each other. When there is competition there is always an opposition. When we compare ourselves with others, it lowers our self-esteem. Self-esteem is the basic context in which we act and react, choose our values, and set our goals. The world is full of contrasts and no one knows what is the instrument of measurement to gauge others. You should compare your self with yourself. One should be better today than yesterday and still better tomorrow. Struggle but do not struggle to stand out.

No Blame Game

Blaming others for our problems is a sign of weakness. One should take full responsibility of one's life and accept problems as opportunities to grow inwardly. It is said that misery is always a greater teacher than happiness. Defeat the problems with all the might. When we suffer at some point of time, we should not feel dejected as the suffering will go away, sooner or later.

Love Yourself

Buddha said that you yourself deserve your love and compassion as much as anybody in the entire cosmos. Love your own company. Be your own friend and guide. You are as important in this universe as anyone else. Identify your good points and develop them to take benefit out of them. This way you also eradicate your shortcomings. When you love yourself, you feel good about yourself. When you feel good about yourself other people suddenly appear nicer.

Be a Thinker

Think critically and creatively. A thinking mind is a positive mind. We should think about how to make the world a less violent place to live in. What can be my contribution to that? Our purpose of life should be to become a socially useful person. Creative thinking means exploring all avenues of the subject of thought so that each thought wave gives new idea. A thinking mind contributes towards inner growth which in turn creates unfailing interest in life. Also when you think, you practise silence, which conserves energy. Think big to act big.

Be Contented

Contentment means acceptance of the present without multiplying our daily wants. Man's happiness really lies in contentment. You are much better off than many others. Contentment brings cheerfulness in one's life. A man of cheerful disposition inspires others to smile. When you realize that you are not lacking in anything, you get the feeling that the whole world belongs to you.

Be a Giver

Practise the art of giving. The joy of giving is many times more than what you get in receiving from others. What you give to others always goes with you. What you take from others stays behind. Become a cause of happiness, peace and harmony for others and never become a cause of suffering to anyone. Lord Krishna says a person who gives no trouble to the world is dear to Him.

Go Universal

Have full faith in the Indian thought that the world is one family—*vasudhaiva kutumbakam.* Believing in the phrase will help develop a sense of belonging to the whole world. You will then have a universal perspective and no one would appear a stranger to you. You will have vision of many in one and one in many as the same divine spirit resides in all. You may love your region or community but you should not get tied down to them. Expand your love to embrace the entire creation. Then you will understand the true meaning of equality. Then you will love diversity and respect all religions of the world. Only a person with a universal outlook can develop a detached outlook since he would not be attached to anything in particular. By all means love your region, community and your country, but your love should not stop at the borders. Be a world citizen without frontiers.

Pray Daily

Through prayers we remain in contact with God. Besides praying for your own good, pray for the welfare of others. Start your prayers with thanking God for all what he has given to you. With prayers one remains in a positive state of mind. When you pray for others you get a reward which is equivalent to the fruit of selfless work. Prayers show us the right way to act.

Be What You Are

There should be no contradiction between your inner life and outer life. Do not pretend and load your mind with artificiality. Make your life an open book where there are no secrets, no falsehood, no malice and no treachery. A truthful person is a simple person who fears nothing. A simple mind can very easily become a positive mind. A simple mind is a selfless mind. If you keep your face to sunshine you will have a positive attitude as you will not see the shadows.

Elevate Yourself

Grow vertically. When you do that you do not bother too much about name and fame. Accept that ultimate goal of life is your spiritual growth. Two great hindrances to self-elevation are laziness and resignation. Laziness makes it impossible to accomplish what you have set as goal and resignation results in giving up before really trying. Be alert and active and do not underestimate your capability. Nothing belongs to man for which he does not strive. Cultivate new positive life-enhancing qualities. Accept new situations, accept others, and change yourself for the good.

Heighten Your Personality

Two very big components of your personality are mind and intellect. Use them to develop an ability to manage yourself. Always count your blessings which shall invariably be more than your sorrows. Have an ideal in life that gives you direction like the two banks of a river allows it to run smoothly. Otherwise, its water will flood all over.

When we are not aware of our capabilities and potential, we feel low about ourselves. With low self-esteem neither we can develop a positive personality nor can we advance on the spiritual path. We have to build up self-esteem to do something worthwhile in life.

Building up Self-Esteem

Self-esteem means feeling good about oneself. It is an understanding that we are worth something regardless of criticism, blame or adverse judgment by others. Self-esteem is the belief that we have the potential to do something good in whatever condition we are placed. It is a feeling of self-worth which convinces us that we can contribute towards the well-being of others. Self-esteem is a firm belief on our personal values on which we stand like a rock without any compromise. When we build up self-esteem we do not require any certificate from others as to how good we are. At our ordinary level of existence we feel better when people tell us what we want to hear about ourselves. We all waste part of our life in attempt to display those qualities which we do not possess. Swami Vivekananda goes to the extent of saying that nine-tenth of our life energy is spent in trying to make people think which we are not. But when we develop self-esteem we do not base our life on the opinion of others and we stay natural as we are. With self-esteem we stay out of artificiality and do not regulate our life to please others.

Self-esteem needs to be differentiated from self-pride or personal ego. When we have self-pride or when we rely on our personal ego, we consider ourselves superior to others and with this feeling we get disinclined to mix up with people around us. A man with self-esteem has no such pride and he reaches out to people with a hand of friendship whosoever they are. He gives comfort to those who come in his contact. You may not be able to control the atmosphere around yourself, but you can better your life by building self-esteem. Only you can decide what you feel about yourself, how to behave and how to stay positive and self-respecting. People will disrespect you when you disrespect yourself. Again people would love you when you love yourself. This is what self-esteem is all about.

The more natural we are, the more self-esteem we shall develop. The more self-esteem we develop the more close we shall move towards self-perfection. When we pretend and make people think of us what we are not, we further move away from our natural state and then feeling good about ourselves remains a distant idea. Other important aspect of building self-esteem is creating some merit within. If nothing else, we should become truthful and pure in our thoughts, words and deeds. It requires no self-effort but just mindfulness refraining from falsehood. As we develop truthfulness, we acquire purity of the heart. With truthfulness comes honesty and straightforwardness and also simplicity that is applicable in all walks of life. A truthful person is held high in the eyes of others.

Love Yourself

Only if you love yourself you can distribute love to others. Self-love is not selfishness. Self-love is self-acceptance, self-appreciation and self-compassion. A bit of appreciation for your own self is needed when you do something good. This is how self-love would grow. When you love others you are bound to receive love from others in higher proportion.

Judge yourself but do not sit on the judgment of others. Judging yourself enables you to find your faults and correct them. One can easily perceive faults of others but to perceive faults of one's own self is difficult. This is because one has a tendency to hide one's faults. When you succeed in overcoming the faults, you start feeling that you are not unworthy and your life is not irrelevant. Then you do not fear obstacles but face them considering them as an opportunity to grow. When you grow your past fades away and you get free to accept new opportunities to uplift yourself. When you develop self-esteem you realize that no one can harm you except you yourself. You also decide how people will behave with you. You gradually develop a consciousness that you are responsible for all that happens to you. It is you who make yourself sad or bright and not circumstances outside you. Only a person with low self-esteem will be affected by outer conditions.

If one is inclined towards religion or spirituality, one's efforts to build self-esteem get a boost. Then you realize that God has ordained a definite role for you. Even if you are not inclined towards religion or spirituality, you can build up self-esteem by relying on your good qualities. When one becomes good, one acquires sincerity and selflessness. Swami Vivekananda said that good motives, sincerity and infinite love can conquer the world. One single soul possessing these virtues can destroy the dark designs of millions of hypocrites and brutes.

An extremely important trait of positive personality is to develop an ability to learn lessons from life and improve upon oneself. Life is a school and the earth is a big class room. Living is for learning and learning makes you knowledgeable and wise.

Live to Learn

Nobody in the world is perfect. We have to learn, unlearn and re-learn throughout our lives. Unlearning means to throw out unnecessary information from our mind. Mark Twain said that education consists mainly of what we have unlearnt. Our motto in life should be—'As long as I live I will learn'. But why should we learn throughout our life? It is to make sure that the knowledge that we acquire while we live is effectively used to negotiate the obstacles we face in life rather than living mechanically and allowing things to happen without our consent. The other advantage of learning is that when we learn continuously we live every moment of life purposefully and not in a routine manner. With learning one keeps oneself engaged and there are no boring spells. We must understand that we have unlimited capacity to learn. Sri Aurobindo says that all life is a school.

Swami Vivekananda said that the goal of mankind is knowledge. Pleasures come to an end and it is a mistake to regard them as your aim of life. Most of us associate process of learning with formal education like going to schools and colleges and appearing in examinations. And when formal education ends, we tend to accept that our learning process has come to an end. This is farthest from the truth. Life is designed to make us grow and become wiser day by day through the process of learning, and when we do not learn we stagnate. It is said that life is a teacher and that too a tough teacher which takes exam first and gives lessons later. How true is this! When we confront hard situations in life, we do learn while dealing with them. What hurts also instructs. We should also not forget that in all of us there is an inherent urge to evolve ourselves and this urge gets a boost when we negotiate problems in life.

What sort of knowledge should we seek to make as our goal of life? Our *Upanishads* state that there are two categories of knowledge. One is objective knowledge which is the knowledge of the world we live in. This knowledge is needed by us and includes scientific knowledge. This is lower knowledge which is also referred as *apara vidya*. The other category of knowledge is subjective knowledge or the knowledge of the self or the spiritual knowledge. This is the deeper dimension of knowledge which is the very ground of our existence. This is higher knowledge which is referred to as *para vidya* or *atma vidya*, the knowledge of the Supreme Reality or the *Brahman*. It is the higher knowledge which shapes our personality and gives us guidance to meaningfully live in the objective world. Our goal in life should be to acquire higher knowledge as well as the lower knowledge. Therefore, man has to continuously learn from both the spheres of knowledge. Lower knowledge helps us to live in the world but by itself it is not complete knowledge. On the other hand, higher knowledge is complete knowledge and is all inclusive. It is the transcendental knowledge. Lower knowledge gives us worldly wisdom whereas higher knowledge gives us spiritual wisdom which is the goal of human life.

What does learning a thing involve? Learning does not mean just knowing something. Learning is a complete understanding of what we have acquired, to an extent that it becomes a part of us. To accomplish this we must have a willingness to learn with an open mind. Throughout our life we keep on learning something or the other which is of no real value to us. This constitutes plenty of unwanted information which fills up our mind. To allow useful things to enter our mind, we should throw out all irrelevant things out to accommodate good things we want to learn. This process of weeding out unwanted information from our mind is referred to as unlearning. Thereafter, we learn what is good for us and we call this process as relearning. To learn new things in life, we must live in the present rather than thinking about our past mistakes or imagining our future. We should consider each day as the first day of our new phase of life. This shall make us feel fresh everyday. Also we must have faith in our ability to learn. Most of us have a tendency to talk more but listen very little. This should be reversed. You should be a good listener and listen to what others say. Those who will listen will learn provided they empty themselves of their petty ego. To be a good learner one has to be perfectly humble without the slightest trace of self-importance.

Aids for Learning

One of the best aids of learning is learning from one's mistakes. Man can learn from his own mistakes provided he does not repeat them. Never leave your mistake unattended. Do we have to look for a teacher or a guru to learn in life? There is only one supreme teacher, that is, God who is present in all of us in the form of our *atma* or soul. So, one should be one's own teacher as far as possible. In the spiritual field one may have a guru in physical form or in the form of a scripture or a holy text. Ramana Maharishi said he is the proper guru to whom your mind is attuned. We can learn so many things out of our life's experience. The Hindu scriptural text, the *Bhagavatam,* talks about sage Dattatreya who called himself a student of nature. He said that *atma* alone was his guru but he had learnt 24 things from elements, animals, and human beings who were also his gurus. From the earth, he learnt patience and doing good to others. From air, he learnt detachment. Air keeps moving through various objects but is attached to none of them. From the deer he learnt not to fall prey to temptations. The deer is trapped by hunter through temptation. From the child he learnt to be free from worries and anxieties. The child always lives in the present and is cheerful. The world as guru reveals all precious secrets of life.

Old Age and Learning

Learning has nothing to do with age provided one has a will to learn. No one is too old to learn. Even if one learns in old age, it is wonderful. Learning adds joy to life which is the most needed in old age. With learning one turns ordinary life into extraordinary. We all have something extraordinary in us which can be manifested by learning. Our aim should be to convert knowledge gained by us into wisdom. Sri Sarada Devi, spiritual consort of Sri Ramakrishna said, "Learn to make the whole world your own. No one is a stranger; the whole world is your own." We must learn this even if we do not want to learn anything else.

The UNESCO gives five principles of learning—Learning to know, Learning to do, Learning to be, Learning to live together, and Learning the treasures within. All these coincide with Swami Vivekananda's definition of education when he said that education is manifestation of perfection inside the man. 'Learning to do' is secular education which enables us to earn our living. 'Learning to be' is sacred learning through which we develop a positive personality inclined towards spirituality. It is through our spiritual inclination that we learn to live together. When we know something thoroughly we should teach it to others. What matters is not what you have learnt but what you have taught. Swami Vivekananda said God is not for those who live for themselves. Living for one's own self is an animal status.

Spirit of Service

A man with a positive approach in life will have an attitude to serve others as service leads to self-elevation. Service to mankind means expressing concern for others, caring for others, and providing help to the needy. Service is one of the ideals of Indian culture and heritage. Showing concern for others is essential for human development as it expands our vision that promotes social health. As per Indian thought, serving society is a means to reach God. Spirit of service refines our inner energy which can be directed towards a noble cause. The attitude of serving others moves us away from selfishness and helps us to acquire virtues such as purity of mind, love and sincerity. That is why it is said that when you get an opportunity to serve others, it should be regarded as a divine grace. It is our humble duty to make a difference to someone's life through our service. When we serve others without any personal motive we demolish our personal ego leading to peacefulness of mind and a sense of togetherness.

Service humanity is given a very high priority in all religions of the world. They teach us to serve others without any personal motive. Hinduism is founded on humanism which is extending benevolence towards human kind. Service and love are central themes of Christianity. Islam holds that serving His creation is manifestation of belief in God. Buddhism asks us to do good to others. Jainism highlights that sufferings of others should be removed through rightful means. Sikhism calls for service to humanity by sharing earnings with the needy and the downtrodden. All religions of the world convey that mutuality and interdependence are means to progress of society since man is not an island and is interconnected with others.

Service to others can be rendered at both physical and mental level depending upon the capability of the server. At the physical level, we can help the needy by giving food and money or visit sick in hospitals and meet their requirements. At the mental level, we can serve others through our useful writings and books which can influence many with whom we have no physical contact. We can even comfort others by our words. Listening to the problems of others is also a service because the one who is in distress is comforted by a patient hearing. We can serve others even by praying for their well-being. To teach healthy ideas to others is also a service which can be given to anyone at any time. All forms of services are good and should be undertaken as per the ability and inclination of the server. Swami Vivekananda said that raising the mind set of the receiver is the best possible service. Giving an eatable to someone would not curb the hunger forever. Similarly, giving clothes to somebody would only solve the problem temporarily as the clothes would wear out with the passage of time and shall require fresh replacement. But if you can remove the ignorance of the receiver by imparting knowledge to him, it would remain his life time companion. Swami Vivekananda emphasized that knowledge empowers man to conduct himself successfully in difficult and different conditions.

Mother Teresa said that there cannot be any true service without love nor can there be real love without service. She further said that hands that serve are holier than the lips that pray. I would further add to it that if you do not get a chance to serve with your hands, praying from lips should not stop. In fact, praying from lips should be done even when we can serve with hands. Whether you serve with hands or pray from lips, it is necessary that we serve others with a feeling of love and equality. Love in service will only develop when we acquire a feeling of oneness with others. One should never serve with a sense of pity for those who are suffering. The *Bhagavad Gita* says that to give is a man's duty and you cannot pity others while you perform your duty. Ramakrishna Paramahamsa expressed similar views when he said that it was one's duty to serve. He said that one should not serve with a feeling of compassion since that could bring in a sense of superiority in the server which would defy the basic concept of service based on equality. He called working for others as the best work which one can do for oneself. Sri Sri Ravi Shankar has the same opinion when he asks mankind to engage in community service to the best of one's ability.

Health of a nation depends upon the quality of individual contribution towards the well-being of the society. India as a developing nation needs people who can render dedicated services to remove the ills of the society. We need men and women who can serve others for the sake of service and not for any personal gains. We all are capable to serve others whatever may be our station and stage in life. It is an incorrect belief that only influential and rich people with resources can give something to the society.

Every individual has some plus points in him which can be utilized for the benefit of others. Our service, however, should not be confined to the members of our own community or to our near and dear ones. No distinction of people, caste or creed should be made when we serve. When we serve only those who are close to us, it does not contribute towards our self-elevation; only selfless service does. It is said that visiting holy places or idol worship dos not purify a man as much as the selfless service of fellow creatures.

Services offered to fellow beings are equivalent to worship of God. Serving others is akin to meditation since you utilize your power of concentration to remove the sufferings of humanity. There are three different attitudes of mind with which one renders service to others. In the first stage we serve others considering it as our duty. In the second stage, we serve because we are devoted to the welfare of others. And in the final stage, we rejoice in welfare of others which accrues out of our service. The third is considered the best. When you seek to reduce the suffering of any fellow creature whether your efforts succeed or not, you evolve closer to spiritually.

Aim of human life is twofold: self-elevation and contribution towards social efficiency. When we serve others we move on the path of self-evolution and at the same time the efficiency of the society is improved by our dedicated and sincere service. When one serves selflessly, one understands the true meaning of the 'duty concept' which is primarily to give and not take. The server develops a loving relationship with all members of the society. So one should be ever ready to give to others cheerfully.

Great men become great not because a position is given to them but they have acquired it rightfully with their sincere, dedicated and selfless service rendered in a spirit of humbleness for the betterment of the human kind. While serving selflessly, one automatically acquires generosity and goodwill towards others and at the same time sheds weaker inclinations. These attributes contribute towards one's character building. Universal outlook accrued as a result of service rendered on the basis of equality brings the distant ones near and makes friends out of strangers.

The highest service to mankind is not to do evil to any one, think evil of anyone, and speak evil of anyone. While rendering service to others, we may have to sacrifice our self-interest. But this is perfectly in order. The *Vedanta* says that for the sake of family sacrifice self-interest, for the sake of country sacrifice family interest, for the sake of world sacrifice country's interest and for the sake of God sacrifice everything. Serving others can be equated with an act of sacrifice. The spirit of service is a spirit of sacrifice (*yajna*) which is a divine attribute. Sacrifice can also be interpreted as a means of self-control and discipline. Every form of self-control where we surrender our ego and where we transcend our lower impulses is also a sacrifice.

Our scriptures inform us that we should possess a detached view in life. It is a very common trait of human nature that when we like a person we like to see him again and again. This is attachment. On the other hand, detachment is freedom from attachment. If we are not detached we do not grow inwardly because attachment to someone limits our vision and thinking. One way out of attachment is by remaining attached to all which conveys the same sense as detachment to all.

Be Detached and Yet Make the World Your Own

It looks a paradox, but it is true that a man with a detached disposition is a friend of all. He dislikes none and is at ease with everyone. We can realize it when we grasp the true purport of detachment. Detachment whose Sanskrit equivalent is *vairagya* is the most essential requisite for spiritual progress as detachment leads to a spiritual outlook. Hindu texts lay utmost emphasis on detachment for self-evolution. Detachment, non-attachment, dispassion—they all convey the same meaning that we should not be drawn towards worldly desires, attractions and temptations. Attachment leads to bondage and detachment to freedom. Attachment is misery, while detachment is enjoyment. Detachment is a mental state which is achieved by relinquishment or *tyaga* of worldly desires and longing for worldly objects. It is not by physical distancing from worldly objects that we can become detached. A person may be in a forest but his mind might crave for sensual objects. On the other hand, a man may be in the midst of worldly life and yet be detached. The idea behind detachment is not clearly understood by a common man. Therefore, it is necessary to understand what exactly detachment is and what it is not.

What Detachment is Not

It is the most common belief that when we keep ourselves aloof from worldly affairs, we acquire a detached outlook. This is not true. Indifference, negligence, neglect of duties, caring for others and becoming unconcerned towards others are not examples of detachment. Detachment is also not absence of sympathy, participation or involvement. Detachment is not living the life of a recluse being totally cut off from worldly affairs.

What Detachment is

Detachment is love and care for all as opposed to attachment where you are connected with specific people. Detachment is an attitude born out of knowledge. It is an act of disengaging the mind from all forms of sensory pleasures. Detachment is living in the world but remaining unaffected and undisturbed by every situation of life. It is a way to live in the world by exercising control over passions and urges. Detachment can be compared to sailing in a boat but not allowing the water to enter the boat. It is like living in the world but not allowing outer conditions to dictate terms. Detachment is living like a lotus in muddy water without being affected by the surroundings. With attachment arises dependence and dependence brings slavery. When the object of attachment is out of reach, one feels miserable. Attachment gives you the idea of possession and gets reflected in expressions such as my car and my house. Conversely, it is detachment when you enjoy the pleasures of life, wealth and status without being dependent on them as things of possession. You act as the master and not servant to these. A detached man develops inner freedom which no one can conquer. While being detached you care for others as human beings. It is feeling of fullness of love without any sense of possession.

There is yet another way of understanding detachment. When you are attached to God wholeheartedly, you are detached to the whole world. Our attachment to God is directly proportional to our detachment to the whole world. When you love everyone in the world, you are attached to the whole world and simultaneously detached to all as you are not attached to specific people. Universal attachment is also detachment. When you are attached to all, you reap the same fruit as when you are detached to all. Universal attachment is perfect detachment and yet the whole world appears as your own. Attachment to God is not wrong but attachment in human relationship results in possessiveness and passion which should be guarded against. Detachment is thus the way to live in the world so that we do not remain aloof and unloving from the rest of the world.

The *Bhagavad Gita* deals with detachment exhaustively. Mind is fickle and difficult to control but can be brought under control by detachment and practice. By working without attachment a man attains the supreme. The scripture defines *karma yoga* as working selflessly with detachment and dedication. Only that person excels who on becoming non-attached lives a life of communion through dedicated action. To remain steadfast in Yoga, one has to abandon attachment. The *Bhagavad Gita* describes the world as an inverted tree with roots above and branches in the lower region. One who is entangled in the world cannot come out of it unless he cuts the firmly rooted world tree with the powerful axe of non-attachment or detachment. Such is the strength and capability of detachment. It argues detachment from family members and with their fortunes as one is only like a managing trustee of his family and nothing beyond that. It asks man to abandon attachment to all material possessions. A man should overcome delusion which springs from attachment to make any worthwhile progress in the spiritual field.

How does one go about to achieve detachment? It is by being attached to all and not being attached only to some specific people. Self-control is a must for securing a detached outlook which can be truly effective if side by side there is inner evolution or inner blossoming. Attachment can be reduced by sidelining situations that cause it. Detachment is a divine attribute and to understand it we have to lean towards the divine. To eliminate attraction and repulsion for sense objects, we have to get rid of our likes and dislikes. We have to develop equal mindedness or sameness of mind towards all situations of life and equal vision towards all whom we meet. When that happens, attachment towards a particular set of people is overpowered, and attachment makes the way for detachment.

Other effective means for developing detachment are meditation, study of scriptures and company of holy people. Detachment is also gained by process of discrimination between right and wrong, real and unreal, and happiness and pleasure. Devotion to God burns all impurities including attachment. But for that, we must have complete faith in God to enable us to take refuge in Him. Patanjali calls attachment as one of the afflictions which must be remedied. Lord Mahavira said that complete detachment from the world is a prerequisite to the practice of non-violence. Detachment presupposes that we are in the normal course attached to the world. This is true also for a very vast majority of us. So when we know what attachment is we strive harder to achieve non-attachment or detachment.

Is there a Need to Compete with Others?

In the world today, everyone is all out to outdo others by competing with them. The world believes in the policy of one-upmanship. One may ask if competing with others is the right way of living. It is certainly not and that is why Indian philosophy stresses on the need to complement and not compete. Do not compete or compare with others. Take part in the race but without looking at others. Everyone is unique and incomparable. Complementing others is the right way to live which encourages man to develop oneness in all existence. The competition should be only between a man's present self and the past self. This is to ensure that the self of present has beaten the self of the past in acquiring higher values of life. Complementing others spreads cooperation, harmony and togetherness and brings unity in diversity. It removes jealousy, envy and separatist tendencies. Competition allows unhealthy practices to slip into the system. Competition is not life even though we see competition all around us. The *Bhagavad Gita* does not favour competition in life. It says that we should be satisfied with whatever comes without calculations. The spirit of complementing others and not competing often takes the expressions such as two sides of a coin, two wings of a bird and two wheels of a cart. Our saints often quoted these to bring home the point that human beings should not compete with each other since they complement and strengthen one another.

Gandhiji called truth (*satya*) and non-violence (*ahimsa*) as two sides of the same coin. Without the one, the other remains incomplete and does not get glorified, he argued. Both truth and non-violence complement each other for lifting man to a higher state of existence provided these virtues are sincerely practised by him. If one is truthful and lives truthfully, he removes a host of evil tendencies from inside including falsity which causes one to act violently. Similarly, if one is non-violent he remains calm and poised. This helps him to manifest truth or the Ultimate Reality from within. Gandhji's devotion and loyalty to truth and non-violence was so great that he made them the focal point of his struggle for gaining independence from the British rule. He proclaimed that not even for the freedom of India he would resort to untruth nor he would purchase India's freedom at the cost of violence. That Gandhiji succeeded in his mission speaks very highly of these two universal virtues.

Swami Vivekananda explained Indian philosophy by giving the example of two wings of a bird. He said that renunciation and service are the twin ideals of India which are like two wings of a bird. Both these ideals are essential for spiritual progress of human beings as two wings are required for a bird to fly. When one renounces selfishness, he can serve others in true sense and when one begins to serve others, he understands what renunciation really means. Renunciation or *tyaga* forms an inseparable part of Indian thought which is generally misunderstood by a worldly man. Renunciation is not discarding worldly life but it is an inner feeling when one is a complete master of his inner life after he has abandoned selfishness, personal ego, attachment, likes and dislikes and established himself on higher and noble values of life. Renunciation is not escapism, but rightful involvement in all activities of life. The more we think in terms of doing good to others, the more we become impersonal and unselfish.

Swami Vivekananda used the simile of two wings of a bird also to represent man and woman who according to him should be treated at par. He highlighted that for a society to progress purposefully and smoothly, women should be given the same status as men since it was not possible for the society to progress if it depended on men alone. Specially so when women constitute almost half the population of humanity. He even said that it is not possible for a bird to fly on only one wing. Swami Vivekananda conceived the idea of creating a centre for women which would serve as a focal point for their progress and would radiate moral and spiritual values. He wanted this centre to revolve around the holy mother Sri Sarada Devi, the spiritual consort of Ramakrishna Paramahansa. Swami Vivekananda ruled out the concept that women cannot pursue spiritual ideal. The brainchild of Swami Vivekananda finally took shape and Sri Sarada Math named after the holy mother Sri Sarada Devi was formally inaugurated in Dakshineshwar in 1954.

Two wheels of a cart is another phrase which is used to convey interrelationship between two identities. Men and women are often described as two wheels of a cart personifying that both men and women should work in unison for the cart of life to run smoothly. Moral of the story is that we should always believe in complementing rather than competing with others. The former brings unity and care where as the latter makes us feel that there is an opposition and leads to disunity and distrust. A man desirous of building a positive personality will never compete with others.

We must have faith in God, the Supreme Power, and at the same time have faith in ourselves. Faith is a unique word.

Its sanskrit equivalent is *shraddha*. Faith is our one hundred per cent trust on God, scripture and also on our own self.

Faith on God is to be Selfless

Faith is our capacity to conceive a goal, visualize it and clearly work out means to achieve it. At our average state of religious understanding, our faith in God is linked with our prayers. We pray to God to obtain something and our faith in God starts developing when we receive the desired object. A feeling comes to our mind that with our faith in God we shall remain under His protection and our request shall be answered by God. But sometimes it may happen that things do not work out for us the way we desire despite the fact that we have faith in God. Then we feel that our faith in God is wavering or has become unsteady. This can happen with most of us and an answer to this is that our faith in God based on give and take is not true faith. Faith in its deepest sense is always selfless but we make it selfish by expecting God to remove our sufferings. We use God as a tool to take us out of our sufferings. Such understanding is based on short-sightedness. Our faith in God should be unwavering and unflinching and should not be shaken up even when things do not happen our way. Faith means placing our trust completely and wholeheartedly irrespective of what happens to us. Faith in God is one of the preconditions for acquiring knowledge and wisdom. Faith in God builds up our faith on our own ability since God resides within us. Swami Vivekananda said that the history of the world is history of few men who had faith in themselves. Tolstoy called faith in us the force of life. Tagore said that faith is the bird that feels the light and sings when the dawn is still dark. Adi Shankara exhorted that understanding based on the words of Guru and scriptures is called faith by which truth is realized. The man may be learned in the *Shastras*, may know many languages but if he is devoid of true faith in God, he is no better than an ignorant man. Faith is not just a trust on God; it is a noble and sacred feeling that comes directly from our heart without any reservations.

Selfless faith in God can also be defined as an inclination of heart toward righteousness. Faith has to be selfless because you cannot turn towards righteousness if you are selfish. It is the pure heart which can have complete faith in God without any personal motive. God never betrays those who have selfless faith in Him. Faith is beyond belief. Belief can be shaken but not faith. Faith is total belief in the unknown as opposed to belief which is faith in the known. Faith when influenced by reason gives insight to a problem and reason inspired by faith improves our efficiency. Faith based on reason saves us from doubts, confusions and temptations.

Faith by itself is refined and pure but when it is mixed up in man's nature, it is affected by the particular mode of nature predominant in man. Faith is rooted in natural disposition of man derived from the impression of previous births. It could be totally good or mixed with passion and ignorance. Faith by itself is the nobler way of life when we are established on the teachings of our scriptures. The *Bhagavad Gita* says that man is made up of his faith and he verily is what his faith is. It explains three kinds of faith, from the highest to the lowest. It further says that the type of faith which a man possesses influences his attitude towards worship; the austerity which he undertakes with body, speech and mind; the food he eats, the sacrifice which he performs and the charity which he gives. True faith in God is universal and not founded in narrow-mindedness. It includes a devotional attitude. Faith precedes devotion and as we further advance in spirituality, faith and devotion move side by side. One thing is absolutely certain that God loves us as per the measure of pure faith in Him. This cannot be explained but experienced. With our ego we cannot achieve much on the spiritual path. But with our complete faith in God selfishness and ego vanish and God's grace descends on us enabling us to progress on the spiritual path. Faith can be build up with sincerity of words and right understanding. Faith lands itself to cheerfulness and is brightened by self-efforts.

Freedom is Life

Freedom is the object of human life. We all love freedom of whatever kind it may be. At our average state of consciousness we do not like to be tied down—not even to the law of the land. But how do we define freedom? Does the same freedom mean different thing to an enlightened as well as an unenlightened person? These are some of the questions we have to answer while discussing freedom. An ignorant person feels that he is ever free to act the way he wants without bothering whether his actions could be harmful to others. On the other hand, for a wise person freedom means freedom from ignorance when his actions are based on knowledge. For a man of wisdom it is not freedom for anything but freedom in the midst of everything.

Swami Vivekananda said that freedom is the goal of human life and it is to be attained by perfect selflessness in thoughts, words and deeds. He emphasized that unselfishness is the key to freedom. If our goal is to attain freedom we must struggle for it. Real freedom is when one has the knowledge that he is free from all forms of limitations irrespective of time and space, when one understands that he is free from all doubts and compulsions. Such freedom is possible only when we try to raise our state of consciousness to the highest level where the divinity inherent in all of us automatically gets manifested. In this state, our freedom is such that we do not fear anything including death. We become free while living, rising above both good and evil. We have no anxiety and no unhappiness whatsoever. We are completely non-dependent on others and we do not lack anything or ask for it. We also acquire the ability to choose what is true and beneficial and reject what is harmful and false.

There are two aspects of freedom—inner and outer. To ensure that our freedom is everlasting and not dependent on outer conditions, the inner freedom must precede outer freedom. Inner freedom means full awareness of the self and the feeling that one is free. In the *Ashtavakra Gita,* it is stated that he who considers himself free is free indeed and he who considers himself bound remains bound. So much depends on your own thought and quality of thinking. Spiritual freedom once acquired is never lost and gradually pushes us closer to outer freedom. Self-regulation and living a disciplined life are the foundations on which we build our inner freedom. The more disciplined we are, the freer we would become. No legislation can make us free unless we make sincere effort to free ourselves through self-evolution. Freedom and discipline might look to be opposite of each other but in.reality they are not, and so they complement each other. He more disciplined you are freer you would be. For being disciplined we have to put up with all sorts of restraints in the beginning. Again, if we live truthfully we unload ourselves of falsity that we generally carry. As Jesus Christ said, "Know the truth and truth shall make you free."

Fear robs us of freedom. At an ordinary level of understanding we are surrounded by different fears, some of those are self-created. When we remain stuck with the body idea in the sense that I am the body and nothing else, we remain fearful. But when we raise ourselves and enter the spiritual kingdom, fearlessness starts coming our way giving us freedom. For countering fear, we must develop deep faith in God. When we surrender to God and resign to His will, we start tasting freedom. The other thing which curtails our freedom is anxiety which could be about our future, health, prosperity and the like. If we gear ourselves up to live in the present and devote full attention to it, our mind shall not turn towards anxiety of the unknown. Even if we face some adversity while living in the present, we can face it with full vigour and concentration. Freedom also means accepting every change that takes place in the society even if the change is not favourable to us.

The law of karma pulsates with the message of freedom. Man has the free will to act as he likes. Freedom does not mean what you say is always right. True freedom is freedom from your own thoughts, beliefs and convictions. You should not be attached to your ideas and must allow other ideas to enter your mind. When there is attachment there is desire and when there is desire there can be no freedom. There is interconnectivity among all living beings and we have to accept and live accordingly with what others say. Another thing which becomes an obstacle to attain freedom is the petty 'I' or our own ego. The ego is our limitation and we must break free from it. Our ego is to be replaced by real I in us that is the universal spirit or the *atma*. True freedom lies in merging our limited conscience with universal conscience which enlarges our vision giving freedom. Expansion is freedom whereas contraction is bondage. As regards freedom of words it has to be ensured that freedom of expression has to be within the limits of courtesy and consideration for other. One of the steps to be taken for attaining freedom is to recognize your own limitations and taking corrective steps to eliminate them. Freedom also means freedom from sense pleasures. The *Bhagavad Gita* says that wise man finds no delight in sense pleasures as they are source of suffering only. Freedom from worldly life does not mean breaking worldly ties. It only means staying in world without being affected by it. At the same time, freedom means not a longing for our divine status which requires man to remain in constant touch with God. It is the bondage to wisdom that gives us total freedom. Man is free in the real sense when he acts from the higher level of his personality. Freedom breaks all the walls that separate us from other beings. Freedom means being borderless. Lord Rama said that as one progresses in the journey of spirituality, the rope of freedom becomes longer. Freedom is a must for spiritual life.

> *Life isn't about finding yourself. Life is about creating yourself.*
>
> ***George Bernard Shaw***

Inspirational Stories of Indian Saints

If you judge people, you have no time to love them.

Mother Teresa

As already stated, Indian civilization has been an unbroken and continuous civilization which has remained in tact despite frequent foreign attacks and foreign rules on Indian soil. While a large number of old civilizations have perished or faded away, Indian civilization and culture stands firm on its foundation. It is chiefly because the foundation of Indian civilization is anchored on spirituality. Scriptures like the *Bhagavad Gita* and emergence of saintly persons on its soil have kept the spiritual heritage of India intact. Indian civilization is ever new, fresh and flourishing. India is essentially spiritual. It is only due to political reasons that India is labelled as a secular state which in true sense of the word is not so. Four religions of the world—Hinduism, Buddhism, Jainism and Sikhism—were born in India while other major religions of the world found their way to our country. It is Indian pluralism based on spirituality which has attracted the foreigners to find peace and solace in India. Indian spiritual thought firmly believes that human race is one extended family—*vasudhaiva kutumbakam.* It also believes in welfare of all beings, not only humans but welfare of all life on planet—*Bahujana hitaya bahujana sukhaya.* Indian spiritual thought has no room for sectarianism, communalism and narrow thinking.

India has seen emergence of saintly and holy persons on its soil from time to time. Whenever there has been a decline in Indian morality, a saint has appeared to uplift the masses through the spirit of moral and spiritual values. Take the example of Adi Shankaracharya who put Hinduism back to its pristine glory. Then we have Swami Vivekananda who put Hinduism or *Vedanta* on the world map during his famous Chicago address. Sri Ramakrishna Paramahamsa dispelled doubts on unity of religions by saying, "As many faiths so many paths." Guru Nanak appeared to spread Hindu-Muslim unity and contributed to strengthen the *Bhakti* movement. In the present times, we have Sri Sri Ravi Shankar who has put India on a high pedestal by establishing Art of Living Foundation across the world. We also have Sri Sathya Sai Baba who is conducting training in education of human values through Sai International Centre and others such centres across the globe.

Any study on spiritual values shall remain incomplete if we do not study our saints and sages who stressed on spirituality.

I have included only a few saints in this chapter; not that others are less important but space does not permit me to include all.

Adi Shankaracharya

The great 8th Century saint Adi Shankaracharya, who is popularly known as Shankara, is regarded as an incarnation of Lord Shiva. He was a renunciate, a philosopher, a devotee and a learned teacher. Shankara was also a literary giant, a writer who wrote commentaries on most powerful Hindu scriptures like the *Bhagavad Gita*, the *Upanishads* and the *Brahma Sutras*. He was a spiritual genius who was the first exponent of the *Advaita* philosophy called non-dualism (or philosophy of oneness). Shankara also wrote *stotras* or devotional songs which revived temple worship. It is for his remarkable contribution of reviving Indian spiritual thought that Shankara is considered an incarnation of wisdom. He had outstanding knowledge, deep devotion and intense spirit of service.

When Shankara was born, Hinduism and Indian culture were decaying. Hinduism was split into innumerable sects with each sect giving its individual doctrine, which confused and confounded the masses. People had become very superstitious and had blind faith in their own sects and cults. Teachings of the *Vedas* and the *Upanishads* were grossly misinterpreted. People believed that the *Vedas* was a scripture meant for practising rituals only. Animal killing had become a common custom for performing *yajnas*. Even Buddhism, which had a strong hold on the Indian people at its inception, had become a neglected religion. In short, there was a complete chaos and confusion in the religious field and people were pushed into complete ignorance of the Ultimate Reality. Shankara changed the line of thinking of the people with his thorough understanding of the religion and logical arguments which were not based on theoretical axioms but entirely on his own experience. He reinterpreted, represented and revitalized Hindu scriptures. Shankara enlightened the masses with his peaceful and loving discourses, discussions and debates based on teachings of the *Vedas*. Shankara is rightly credited with the re-establishment of Hinduism which also drove out Buddhism as a church from the country where it was born, though the message of Buddha still transforms lives of many Indians.

As per Shankara's *Advaita* philosophy, reality of *Brahman* is one without a second which cannot be regarded as personal. *Brahman* is the only reality which transcends all distinctions. *Brahman* can only be experienced since it is unthinkable, unperceivable and inexpressible. According to Shankara, *Brahman* and individual soul are identical. This can only be realized when the wisdom arises and the ego is dissolved. Regarding man's true nature Shankara says that you are neither in bondage, nor struggling to break your ties and nor a seeker who is striving for liberation. Neither you are born nor you will die—That you are *(tat tvam asi)*. Man is a reflection of God Almighty, an expression of wisdom and purity. To act without knowledge is sheer ignorance. Shankara describes the world as illusion. He says that world is but a dream, as seen in the mirror. They seem to exist outside ourselves due to ignorance of perception. In reality, all things spring from Self. *Brahma satyam jagat mithya* means *Brahman* is real, world an illusion. Shankara regards action as a means for purification of mind and when wisdom is attained, action falls away. He says that wisdom and action are mutually opposed as light and darkness. Shankara also does not believe in the Vedic rituals and rites which he finds are meant for only those who are lost in ignorance and desire. Practice of rituals is only half job done; know and understand God, the unparallel one. About learning, Shankara says that learning is not a race; all wisdom comes at its own pace with Guru's grace. Talking about Ochre Robes, Shankara says that they are nearly a disguise to fill belly. In his masterly work on devotion, *Bhaja Govindam*, Shankara warns against desire which has many faces and phases and says that one should not be enchanted with worldly attraction. Company of pure helps to overcome them. Shankara also founded monastic order and four *maths* (monasterics) in four directions of India. According to Shankara, three things are necessary for liberation. These are human birth, intense longing for God and divine grace.

Sri Ramakrishna Paramahamsa

Sri Ramakrishna Paramahamsa is one of the foremost spiritual leaders of modern age. He was not a philosopher in the conventional sense, yet he taught highest truths from his spiritual experience. He propagated his philosophy through conversations with his disciples, which were later recorded as Gospel of Ramakrishna, sayings of Ramakrishna and teachings of Ramakrishna. Ramakrishna called the God as Absolute *Brahman* when he is inactive. But when He is involved in the process of creation, preservation and destruction, he is called *Ishvara*, *Shakti* or *Kali*. *Brahman* and *Shakti* are one, just as fire and its burning power are one. Ramakrishna said that God is both absolute and personal. Belief in the one implies belief in the other. Ramakrishna accepted *Maya* as the veil that keeps God hidden from our sight in the same way as a small patch of cloud can hide the big sun from our view.

Regarding good and evil, which is much debated in all philosophies, Ramakrishna says that the ultimate solution is to transcend both good and evil. He said that all religions are true and can be realized by various paths as taught by world religions. Ramakrishna not only practised Hindu religion but also Islam and Christianity to attain highest mystical experiences through them. He gave the example of a water tank which has got many ghats. The Hindus take water from it and call it *jal*. The Muslims take water from another ghat of the same tank and call it *pani*; the Christians take water from the third ghat of the same tank and call it water. Ramakrishna further asks that if someone would argue that the substance is not *jal* but *pani* or not *pani* but water, it would sound very ridiculous. So, why should men quarrel in the name of religion and sects when it is the same God which is called by different names. Different religions are like different staircases to reach the top of the house.

Once you reach the top, you see the same stars, moon and sun. As many faiths, that many paths to reach God. Ramakrishna saw the Divine in all beings and he treated all human beings with respect irrespective of their caste, creed or race. No wonder that Swami Vivekananda spoke of his master Ramakrishna as a man whose life was a parliament of religions.

Ramakrishna advised the mankind not to care for doctrines and dogmas but to care for spirituality which is the essence of existence. He asked mankind to serve others as service of human beings is the service of God as God dwells in all. He said that not compassion but service to the mankind is the way to help the world and attain salvation. Mahatma Gandhi observed that Ramakrishna was a living embodiment of Godliness. His sayings are not those of a mere learned man but they are pages from the book of life. His love knew no limits.

On purity of mind, Ramakrishna said that sunlight is one and the same wherever it falls but only bright surfaces like mirror and polished metal reflect it fully. So divine light falls equally and impartially on all hearts but only pure and clean hearts of holy people can fully reflect it. Like all great spiritual leaders, he was a staunch believer of equality or equal vision which he explained with the help of an example. A man who is on the plains sees the lowly grass and mighty trees thinks how big is tree and how small is grass, but when he climbs up the mountain and looks down on grass and tree, they look one indistinguishable mass of greenery. Similarly, in the eyes of a worldly man, one is a king and the other is a cobbler. But when his level of consciousness is raised, all appear equal and there remains no distinction of good, bad, high or low. After passing away of Sri Ramakrishna, his chief disciple Swami Vivekananda founded RK *Math*, a monastic order and RK Mission where their monks do social service reinforcing Ramakrishna belief that service to mankind is service to God.

Sri Sarada Devi

Sri Sarada Devi, the spiritual consort of Sri Ramakrishna, is worshipped as holy mother from her very birth. She had been pure and a great devotee herself. The concept of motherhood of God and worship of God as divine mother forms a special feature of Hinduism. The *Taittiriya Upanishad* says, "Honour thy mother. Look her up as God." Divine mother is called *Shakti*, the core potency of *Brahman* that projects and preserves the universe. She functions through both knowledge and ignorance.

After passing away of Sri Ramakrishna, Sri Sarada Devi came into limelight with her spiritual insight and wisdom which attracted a large number of devotees. She acquired the role of a mother, teacher and divinity. Holy mother's life was an example of true renunciation. She was not attracted to anything worldly. Sri Sarada Devi treated all, young and old, good and bad, rich and poor alike, exemplifying fine equal vision which is propounded in the *Bhagavad Gita*. She often said, "I am the mother of wicked, mother of virtuous; whenever you are in distress, say to yourself I have a mother. I cannot contain myself when one draws near me and calls me mother." Sri Sarada Devi said time and again that the aim of life was to realize God and remain immersed in His contemplation. She said that path leading to God is difficult in the sense that it is natural for a man living in the word to forget God. Hence, God realization is a slow progress which may extend to many lives. Desire is the man obstacle to God realization. The more intensely one practises spiritual discipline, more quickly he attains good. One should desire God's desirelessness. Love of God is essential for spiritual progress. As wind removes clouds, name of God destroys worldliness.

Sri Sarada Devi always advised her devotees, whether monks or householders, to lead an active life. Man should pray to God to get His blessings and work as long as he lives without accepting anyone's help. She emphasized on genuine self-effort to self-surrender for obtaining divine grace. Her teachings were simple and easily understandable. She referred to pain and sorrow as a means to realize God. People do not realize that grief itself is a gift from God. She accepted that difficulties do come but they do not last forever. They pass away like water through a bridge. Regarding purity of mind, holy mother says that if you want peace of mind, do not find faults in others. Instead, see your own faults and rectify them. She was of the view that the effect of what was to happen as per one's fate could be diluted if one was a true devotee of God. She says that one should learn to make the whole world as his own. No one is a stranger; rather the whole world is our own. This underlines the essence of the

Vedantic thought that the world is a family. This was her final message to the mankind. Time and again, Indian saints have testified this which makes Indian spiritual thought borderless.

Swami Vivekananda

We may call Swami Vivekananda a patriotic saint, a *yogi*, a spiritual leader par excellence, a philosopher, a great thinker and a social reformer. Even such adjectives cannot fully describe him since he possessed so many other remarkable qualities which one knows only after studying his speeches and writings. He was an apostle of activism. He was a beacon light to the youth and it is for this reason that Government of India announced 12th January, the birthday of Swami Vivekananda, as the National Youth Day to be observed all over India; since the philosophy of Swamiji and the ideals for which he lived and worked could be a great source of inspiration to the Indian youth.

Swami Vivekananda is considered to be a foremost Hindu leader who placed Hinduism or the *Vedanta* philosophy—the oldest system of philosophy in the world—on the world map when he attended the Parliament of Religions at Chicago in 1893. In his opening remarks, Swamiji said, "I am proud to belong to a religion which has taught the world both tolerance and universal acceptance. We believe not only in universal toleration but we accept all religions as true." He once remarked that let everyone has his own religion. So what as long as one is moving towards the same God. His closing remarks at the Parliament of Religions were equally impressive when he said, "Help and not fight, assimilate and not destroy." Swami Vivekananda believed in cross fertilization of different cultures of the world which is the very essence of the Indian thought that the world is one family.

According to him, an ideal society is a kind of well-knit family where individual life is the life of the world, where individual happiness is the happiness of the whole. Swami Vivekananda was of the view that manliness of the West should be co-opted with the saintliness of the East for far reaching effects. Gandhiji said that after reading the complete works of Swami Vivekananda, his love for India has increased a thousandfold. Tagore said that if you want to know India, study Swami Vivekananda. There was everything positive and nothing negative in him. Nehru had remarked that he was powerfully influenced by Swami Vivekananda from whom spirit and fire glow out. Younger generations can learn a lot through his speeches and writings. Romain Rolland, who recorded his speeches, said that reading Swami Vivekananda produces thrill like an electric shock through his body.

"Arise, awake and manifest divinity within since you are potentially divine," is the essence of Swami Vivekananda's teachings. According to him, the sole objective behind education and religious movement was to make a man a complete man. He said that it is a sin to call a man sinner since there is divinity inside the man waiting for its manifestation. He gave intense practicality to religion. Swamiji openly declared that Indian culture was deep rooted in religion, which forms the very core of Indian heart. For him, religion was not dogmatism or narrow-mindedness but realization of God in man. Essentially, Vivekananda was a religious man but with a spiritual outlook, and at the same time, his religion did not confine to rituals or sects. Though he worked for the revival of Hinduism, he accepted and revered all other religions. Vivekananda became an outstanding personality through the teachings of his preceptor Ramakrishna Paramahamsa who taught him that service to humanity was equivalent to worship of God. Swamiji placed renunciation (*tyag*) and service (*seva*) as the foremost ideals of India. He defined renunciation as a constant movement towards own highest state of being. According to Swamiji, a spiritual person does not believe in the game of one-upmanship.

Swami Vivekananda coined the term 'Practical *Vedanta*'. He said that time has now come that we make the *Vedanta* or Hinduism practical. Religion is no more a secret living with monks in caves and forests. Religion has to be brought down to the daily everyday life of people. It has to be worked out in all planes of human being. The *Vedanta* is not a religious creed or dogma which people may accept out of fear. It is a timeless quest of human soul for eternal and infinite. Enquiries conducted by ancient sages of India on mystery of life and existence, death and consciousness are much like research conducted by ancient Greeks, modern scientist and the western thinkers relying on external observation. Indian saints relied on inner concentration called Yoga. The record of this was transmitted by Indian saints to their disciples, which is known as the *Upanishad*. The *Vedanta* stands for body of eternal truth comprising laws of spiritual world. The *Vedanta* is the science of self-management for cultivating inner resources.

Swami Vivekananda had a special message for the youth of India. He said that what India needed was young men with muscles or iron and nerves of steel. He wanted youth to develop physical strength, moral purity and mental discipline. He said that youth would be nearer to heaven through football than study of the *Bhagavad Gita* because youth would understand the *Bhagavad Gita* better with their biceps and muscles a little stronger. For regeneration of India, Swamiji wanted young men who could devote their heart and soul to come forward for raising the masses of India. He had passion for improving the conditions of poor masses for which he wanted youth to take part in poverty alleviation programmes, considering it as their duty. Swami Vivekananda opined that our fate was in our own hands. He said that we had the power to make ourselves whatever we wanted to be. If we have been the result of our past actions, it follows that whatever we wish to be in future can be produced by our present actions provided we know how to act. This is a very powerful message for the youth of India from Swami Vivekananda who defined strength as life and weakness as death.

When we examine the present state of our youth, we find them more impulsive and less rational. Due to increasing consumerism, youth are never contended with what they possess and they want more of everything on the materialistic plane. This results in their lack of attention towards developing inner qualities including mental discipline because they do not make any effort to conceive any role model for themselves. Parents and teachers have to pay better attention on providing opportunities to the youth to develop their leadership qualities. What is needed is a holistic approach to build physical, emotional, intellectual and spiritual qualities of the youth or the qualities of hands, head and heart as Swami Vivekananda desired. It is not one day's effort to be undertaken on 12 January of every year, but it has to be a continuous national movement to transform youth into a body of responsible citizens. This requires their moral elevation including building up qualities that define character like loving, caring and sharing. Only when youths develop themselves internally, the life will become dynamic, active and regulated enabling them to undertake the task of improving the conditions of the masses as envisaged by Swami Vivekananda.

Swami Vivekananda could speak on any subject under the sun as he had vast knowledge of everything and anything. He called India an ancient land where wisdom made its home before it went to any other country. He also had realized that the problems in India were more complicated than the problems in any other country because of its size and the divisive tendencies. But he still held the view that India could conquer the world not by physical force but by her spiritual strength. He said that irrespective of whether we believe in spirituality or not, for the sake of national life, we have to get a hold on spirituality and keep to it. According to him, only a spiritual outlook can bring about progress of humanity. He identified himself with the whole world which is quite evident from his lectures and conversations. Swami Vivekananda founded Ramakrishna Mission in 1897 to spread the message which he received from his great teacher after whose name the mission was started.

For strengthening the moral fibre of our society and for turning India into a bright star of the present global village, we need not wait for another Vivekananda to arrive. All we have to do is to locate people with deep sense of loyalty and concern for human welfare to form the nucleus in shaping a new world order where India would play a pivotal role in uplifting the masses based on the teachings of its sages and scriptures. We can follow the example of Sri Aurobindo who wanted spirituality of India or the East to be wedded to the scientific temperament of the West to root out social evils like poverty and illiteracy. His message of love, divinity of man, selfless service, renunciation and truthfulness can lead us from ignorance to knowledge, untruth to truth and death to immorality.

Guru Nanak

Guru Nanak the founder of Sikh religion was a universal man whose simple teachings left a deep imprint on Indian masses. He was a great humanist and a pious global teacher. Universal brotherhood was his creed. He was born at a time when people had totally neglected spiritual realities. Society was split into sectarian groups. People were totally inclined towards rituals which resulted in steep decline of human values and true understanding of religious tenets. Nanak gave the message of oneness on the basis of equality and brotherhood. According to him, a true religious person is one who regards all men and women as equal in all spheres of life. He said that men and women are equal in the eyes of God.

Guru Nanak was a profound thinker, philosopher, revolutionary saint and social reformer. Swami Vivekananda said of Guru Nanak that he preached marvellous love for the world with his broad heart and arms outstretched to embrace the whole world. This is a big tribute to Guru Nanak from a man whose criticism spared none who was not above board.

Guru Nanak believed in one Absolute God whom he attributed as formless, just, loving, righteous and desires to be worshipped through love and righteousness. There is one God who is higher than gurus. He is God of all and not for this and that race, this or that nation, or this and that religion. On the basis of this truth, we should respect all religions. He openly denounced idol worship because he did not limit the God head in any one incarnation. He said that even when we worship an image, make a pilgrimage to a shrine or take a dip in holy water, if the mind is impure, all is in vain. He was highly critical of rituals and caste system. Filth on hands, feet and body may be washed off with water but the mind filled with sin and evil can only be cleansed by devotion to God.

Guru Nanak was highly critical of performance of rituals. He encouraged debates on rituals by performing such acts which would attract criticism from public who practise rituals. He once prepared meat at Kurukshetra. When objected by others, Guru Nanak said that God was equally present everywhere and therefore Kurukshetra had no special significance for him where he should not cook meat. At Haridwar, Guru Nanak saw people splashing water from River Ganga in a particular direction. When Nanak asked the reason for this act, he was told that they were doing so to ensure that the water reaches their dead ancestors resting in celestial spheres. Hearing this, Nanak started throwing water in opposite direction. When questioned, Nanak said that he was doing so, so that the water reaches his fields at his home town. People ridiculed Nanak by saying how could water from Haridwar reach his fields located so far away. To this, Nanak replied that if their water from Haridwar could reach their ancestors located millions of miles away, then how come his water could not reach his fields located only a few hundred miles away from Haridwar.

Guru Nanak called love the highest virtue. His message was that one should work, worship and share one's good with others. He rated truth a very high virtue, but felt that still higher is truthful living. He considered respecting others a high quality, but respecting views of others a higher one.

The three essentials laid down by him for the progress of soul to the God are *Satguru* (True Master), *Satsangat* (Holy Assembly) and *Satnam* (taking God's name). Remembering God and service to humanity are two essentials of spiritual life. Those who serve without seeking return shall find union with God. If you can make someone happy, happiness will come back to you manyfold. There is no need to go to forest in search of God. Live in the world following the path of truth to reach God. Our birth is the fruit of our actions but salvation is by His grace. He placed utmost emphasis on self-control. He said that the true test of a man and woman is to live passionless amidst all passions.

Guru Nanak was the first spiritual leader of India who attempted to establish dialogue with different faiths. He was the first spiritual leader who tried to achieve religious integration. He travelled to Mecca, Medina and Baghdad for promoting unity of faiths and to achieve religious integration. He taught that one should have unqualified respect for all religions and all divine revelations. It is a straightforward acknowledgement of pluralism. That is why Sikhs made the *Guru Granth Sahib,* a pluralist scripture.

Nanak gets the credit of announcing religious pluralism as early as in 15th Century which has now been said in the world over as a result of globalization. He was the first to give a call of Hindu-Muslim unity: "There is no Hindu, no Mussalman." He refused to accept differences in individuals on account of their religion or faith.

Nanak gave a new hope to downtrodden on the basis of equality and brotherhood. According to him a true religious person is one who regards that all are equal. It is not for nothing that Guru Nanak is referred to as world's early socialist.

Guru Nanak's name is associated with the revival of *Bhakti* cult in India. He had complete disregard for meaningless rituals which were prevalent in his time. This is akin to what Lord Krishna said in the *Bhagavatam,* "If a man disregards and persecutes fellow beings but worships Me in images and with numerous rituals, I'm not at all pleased with him for offering such worship."

Sri Aurobindo

Sri Aurobindo whose birth anniversary falls on 15 August was a poet, philosopher, visionary, great patriot, a revolutionary and a *yogi* of the highest order. He is also addressed as an interpreter of Indian culture and spirituality. As a revolutionary, in early part of his life, he changed the entire thinking of Indian freedom struggle through his editorial comments in a newspaper which he himself edited. Aurobindo is considered a great pioneer of Indian renaissance. For his anti-British activities for India's freedom, Aurobindo was sent to jail for one year where he had his first spiritual experience. With this experience, he was convinced that time for India's freedom had not yet arrived. Aurobindo then withdrew from the political scene and came to Pondicherry in 1910 to concentrate on Yoga which he had earlier practised while in jail. During his stay in Pondicherry till his passing away in 1950, Aurobindo wrote on a number of religious and spiritual topics like Yoga, the *Bhagavad Gita*, the *Upanishad* and Indian culture. His books have been translated in a number of languages and he is known for his writings throughout the world.

Aurobindo's strength, though largely intuitive, rests on the *Vedas*, the *Upanishads*, the *Bhagavad Gita* and the Tantric texts. Aurobindo's philosophy and spirituality revolved around the concept of India as mother. He worshipped India as Divine Mother and started his *sadhana* for redeeming her honour. Aurobindo's *sadhana* starts where the others' end. According to him, once the union with the Supreme is realized, one must bring down that realization to the external world and change the condition of life upon the earth until a total transformation is accomplished. Aurobindo believed that man on earth is a transitional being and is not a final product. Man has to rise above his mental state to a super mental state—a state which is higher than individual consciousness. The integral Yoga which Aurobindo preaches seeks divine realization not for the sake of the individual but something to be gained for earth's consciousness.

Aurobindo regards world as real and recognizes no duality between spirit and matter. For this reason, he directs Yoga towards earth's consciousness more than individual divine consciousness. According to him, the spirit descends as super mind on mind, life and matter and matter through *sadhana* ascends to the Supreme Self or *Brahman*. Consciousness involves first in the matter and then matter evolves back to consciousness. Since the world is called real by Aurobindo, it is the real world which is seeking the Ultimate Reality.

Aurobindo believed that God descends when man ascends. To practise integral Yoga as taught by him, a strong aspiration is necessary for a man to raise himself to higher state of existence which would enable him to reject the movements of his lower nature. Rejection of movements of lower nature at physical level would mean getting rid of unwillingness to change for the better; at mental level it is rejection of all ideas that are non-divine and at the vital level it would mean rejection of desires, demands, passion, selfishness, pride, arrogance, jealousy and envy. Aurobindo emphasized that aspiration for raising oneself to a higher level of consciousness can be achieved by study of scriptures which evolves one's thought process. In the integral Yoga, the Divine Himself becomes one's Guru which becomes a reality when man surrenders to God. Integral Yoga calls man to practise together the three Yogas of the *Bhagavad Gita*—work, love and knowledge.

According to Aurobindo, human evolution to a higher and larger consciousness can only be achieved when man gives consent to change his nature he is born with. When a man individually decides to change his nature, then the change can be brought about for uplifting the collective life on earth. Such change can bring an era of divine life on earth. It is not departure out of world but it is something which is gained on earth. It is to bring about radical change on earth by own salvation to start with.

Aurobindo called all life as Yoga and all life a school where learning process never ends. To practise Yoga, man must have unshakable faith in himself because God dwells in him. Aurobindo warns that if one does not have the courage to face worldly life, he will perpetually remain a source of misery and suffering and will never be able to go through the greater inner difficulty of changing his own nature to elevate himself. Faith is not confined to just believing in religion, dogmas or teachings of the master. Faith is the convinced feeling that whatever obstacles, imperfections and rejections are within, one will not forget that one was born for self-realization and one would accomplish that, come what may. Aurobindo called faith a bird that feels the light and sings when the dawn is still dark.

Aurobindo is called voice of Indian soul. He had unparalleled trust on India's ability to transform the entire human race. He proclaimed that India alone can give spiritual gift to the world. India cannot perish, India cannot become extinct because among all divisions of mankind it is India that is reserved the highest and the most splendid destiny, the most essential to the future of human race. It is for India to harmonize all religions, sciences and philosophies which can make mankind one soul. He called Indian culture as highest and noblest in the world as its every activity is directed towards divine. Aurobindo wanted India to be reborn to achieve highest goal because her birth is demanded for future of the world. Aurobindo believed that nations and societies like individuals have body, life, aesthetic temperament, developing mind and even soul. If individuals can transform themselves then why not the nations, he asked.

Aurobindo had great love for India not only because it was his country but because he could see in India what was totally absent in the West where he spent early part of his life. However he said that we should not shy away from the western ideas and harmonize them for achieving unity.

Aurobindo's philosophy for gaining a higher consciousness is directed towards each and every individual and not for chosen ones. If we as individuals can remove our own shortcomings, the shortcomings of the society automatically stand removed making earth a better place to live. In the present era of globalization where there are no obstacles in the flow of knowledge around the globe, India's ability as a world reformer as conceived by Aurobindo, will soon become a reality. Aurobindo did not favour India remaining isolated from rest of world which is in conformity with the Indian thought that world is one extended family. I am always reminded of what Sri Aurobindo said once, "If you are unfit for the world then you are also unfit for God."

Ramana Maharishi

Ramana Maharishi is one of the great sages of India who lived in Twentieth Century. His mere presence among his devotees made enormous impact on them. His *ashram* still exists in South India where not only Indians but also foreigners come and sit before his life-size portrait to feel his powerful presence. Maharishi Ramana did not talk much as he used to observe silence for very long periods. Yet he always replied to the questions put forward by his devotees by writing the answers on a piece of paper.

The substance of Sri Ramana's teachings is Who Am I. He said that self-enquiry leads directly to self-realization. He said that there are no two minds—one good and the other evil —the mind is only one. It is the residual impressions that are of two kinds—auspicious and inauspicious.

When the mind is under the influence of auspicious impressions it is called good, and when it is under the influence of inauspicious impressions, it is regarded as evil. When the mind becomes one, pointed self-inquiry becomes easy. And when the enquiry, Who Am I, is persistently pursued, all other thoughts get destroyed, and finally even the 'I' thought vanishes, leaving the Supreme Non-dual Self alone. The false identification of the self with body and mind thus ends and there is illumination. This is self-realization or God-realization which all spiritual practices teach. This is more of experience than explanation. When you say I am the doer, you bear the consequences of your actions, but when you surrender to God, His grace descends on you and even your destiny would not affect you. Sri Ramana is of the opinion that truth, God and Guru are not different. But he also says that God and Guru will only show the way but will not by themselves take the soul to the state of liberation. The disciple has to work hard on himself to tread the path shown by the Guru. He also says why to see God for a while when you can have a feeling of Godliness at all times. Therefore, one should fill up the mind with thoughts of God. God will act favourably to you when you are striving for goodness. When you seek to reduce the sufferings of fellow creatures whether your efforts succeed or not you will always evolve spiritually.

Not seeking what is other than the Self is desirelessness and not leaving the Self is wisdom. About giving to others, Sri Ramana says that all that one gives to others one gives to one's own self. If this truth is understood who will not give to others. This thought leads to understanding of oneness of all existence. When one of the disciples asked Sri Ramana if he could help the world, he replied that by helping yourself, you help the world. You are the world. If you improve yourself, the world will also improve. Sri Ramana impressed, on others not to be lured by miracle making powers. He advised his devotees to reach the highest through self-surrender only.

Once to answer a query, Ramana Maharishi wrote on a piece of paper, "What will not happen will never happen whatever effort one may put forth and what has to happen will not fail to happen however much one may seek to prevent it." He also sometimes wrote in prose mainly to meet specific demands of his devotees. Ramana Maharishi selected and reinterpreted certain verses of the *Bhagavad Gita* which gives the quintessence of this great scripture. On visiting his *ashram*, one of the foreigners said that he had not seen God even though he is aware of His divine qualities. It is only after coming to India and coming in contact with saints like Ramana Maharishi that he had realized what God could be.

Lal Ded—Spiritual Poetess of Kashmir

Kashmir, which is often described as an abode of saints, has produced a number of pious persons. Among them Lal Ded, who is also called Lalla Yogeshwari, is called the great mystic poetess of the Fourteenth Century. She is regarded as the greatest Apostle of light and love that Kashmir has ever known. She was an ardent practitioner of Kashmir Shaivism which is also known as the *Trika Shastra* founded by Vasu Gupta. Lal Ded took Shaktipat Diksha from her Guru, Sedamol. She was married at a young age but was ill-treated by her husband and particularly by her mother-in-law which prompted her to renounce worldly life to tread the spiritual path. It was from a state of despondency that Lal Ded turned her mind towards God. Her spiritual pursuit commenced with a note of uncertainty which she admits herself. But as she progressed she claimed to have realized Lord Shiva and become a *jivan mukta*—a liberated soul while living.

Lal Ded gave expression to her mystic and poetic inclinations through her *vaakhs* which are four-line poetic verses in Kashmiri. In her *vaakhs,* she covers a vast area of spirituality—Religion, Kashmir Shaivism and even the *Vedanta*—when she says that she is reading the *Bhagavad Gita* at every moment of her life. She was also influenced by Sufism. Lal Ded's *vaakhs* have a universal appeal that catch attention of ordinary mortals as well as spiritually advanced persons. Her *vaakhs* even catch the attention of less sophisticated people of the countryside who sing these *vaakhs* for their inner happiness while working in their fields. Her *vaakhs* are a source of inspiration which touch the depth of the heart and distinctly appeal to the intellect.

Lal Ded's *vaakhs* are so potent with their deep meaning that they have drawn towards them a number of scholars and spiritually inclined people. A total of 138 *vaakhs* which are recognized as authentic have been commented upon by scholars including some western scholars. Each one of them has derived his own meaning out of her *vaakhs* like different *yogis* and scholars who have written commentaries on the *Bhagavad Gita* from different angles and viewpoints.

From a deeper study of her *vaakhs* one can draw the inference that Lal Ded was well-versed in all branches of Yoga including *Kundalini* Yoga. She did not compose her vaakhs as a deliberate contribution to literature or philosophy. Lal Ded was also not a preacher or reformer as such. Her *vaakhs* are mainly outpourings of her soul and an expression of inner experience on what she observed around her. Her central theme was that she was able to realize Lord Shiva within her own self. In one of her *vaakhs,* Lal Ded says, "Chanting Om maddened with love, I set out in his search. I roamed about days and nights. My most auspicious moment came when I discovered my Lord encored within my own heart." This is exactly what Lord Krishna states in the *Bhagavatam,* "People worship Me in images without realizing that I dwell in their heart." Lal Ded called Shiva as the only Reality and the world an illusion which is also the standpoint of the *Advaita Vedanta.*

In her final state of bliss, Lal Ded says, "Whatever I do becomes worship of my Lord. Whatever I speak becomes a *mantra* and each of my breath becomes a *sadhna.*" This reflects her complete spiritual competency resulting in union with the Divine. Lal Ded was much opposed to the rigidity of religion and performance of unnecessary time consuming rituals. She rejected social religious rites, rituals, dogmas, telling of beads, fasting, idol worship and even dip in sacred waters. She declares that God is everywhere and can be found by spiritual practices like deep and silent meditation which she called a *mantra* to reach God. She advised humans not to leave home but stay where they are to find God. She says that wandering *sanyasis* go from shrine to shrine seeking Him who abides within his own self.

In her *vaakhs*, Lal Ded speaks on equality and oneness of all existence, service to mankind, purity of mind and self-control. She gives a beautiful simile to express self-control when she says that one should not give a long rope to the donkey which can make it graze in the field of others. The donkey referred in this *vaakh* is the mind and long rope symbolizes lack of self-control. This conveys not only the significance of self-control but also advises not to covert things that belong to others. She says that the uncontrolled mind would be running in five streets like a thief; five streets being the five senses. Lal Ded advises humankind to remain alike in happiness and misery, honour and dishonour. In one of her *vaakhs,* she says, "Let abuses come to me from all sides still I will not harbour any ill will towards those who abuse me."

Lal Ded did not teach us to escape from life. In one of her *vaakhs,* she advises mankind to 'arise and ascend with karmas.' She believed in the concept of liberation while living. She says that if we cannot realize Him in our lifetime, how can we see Him after death. Lal Ded admits that God is same to all beings. She questions if the Sun will not shine alike at all places instead of giving heat only to holy people and places. It is for this reason that she never differentiated between a Hindu and a Muslim, the two major communities of Kashmir of her time. She was equally revered by both Hindus and Muslims. Lal Ded called supernatural powers as fraud as they, according to her, have no spiritual value. She says that he who regards others as own self, he alone sees the highest good. She further emphasized that by taking God's name, worldly passions vanish like mirage in desert.

There is plenty of similarity between Lal Ded's *vaakhs* and verses of the *Bhagavad Gita*. Like the *Bhagavad Gita,* Lal Ded's *vaakhs* lay down a moral code and provide rules for spiritual advancement. Again like the *Bhagavad Gita,* Lal Ded gives a call to ascend to a higher level of growth while performing one's duties in the world. It would be valid to state that Lal Ded's *vaakhs* act as a beacon light to the entire mankind. The comparative study of the verses of the *Bhagavad Gita* and Lal Ded's *vaakhs* throws light on the compatibility and affinity between the *Vedanta* and Kashmir Shaivism. This establishes that all religious philosophies speak of similar ideals and deeper we go into them more similarity we would find. This also underscores that all religions are same in spirit even though they may appear different in letters.

Lal Ded calls to grow while performing one's duty is the need of the hour. It was not that she was only interested in action. Lal Ded also emphasized on knowledge by saying, "Dress yourself in the clothes of knowledge." Action and knowledge are the only two paths for the humanity which Lord Krishna also underlines in the *Bhagavad Gita*.

Bhagavan Gopinathji

Bhagavan Gopinathji, the Twentieth Century Kashmiri saint, shines like a big bright star among the saints and sages of Kashmir. He is also referred to by his devotees as Bhagavan since he possessed all the six attributes namely knowledge, wealth, power, beauty, fame and renunciation which are associated with this word. Though Gopinathji was a practitioner of Kashmir Shaivism, he was highly influenced by the *Bhagavad Gita* which according to him could serve as one's guru. Not only that, he said that any single verse of the *Bhagavad Gita* could perform guru's job. Such a tribute to the *Bhagavad Gita* can only be paid by a perfect saint possessing universal outlook in whose eyes

The *Vedanta* and Shaivism are not different in essence. It is not for nothing that Gopinathji is addressed as Jagad Guru or world teacher by his devotees. Gopinathji proclaimed that we should think of *Brahman* as a tree. If we sit on any of its branches representing Shiva, Narayan or any other God's head we shall achieve the same goal that is God realization. This is in conformity with an all important verse of the *Bhagavad Gita* where Lord Krishna states, "As men approach Me so I accept them; men follow in every way of my path." Gopinathji firmly believed that saints must help the weak and needy. To those who study scriptures, his advise was that one should live the teachings of scriptures otherwise it is of no use.

Gopinathji said that a spiritual aspirant must first possess three virtues which are straightforwardness or uprightness, purity of mind including clarity of thought and truthfulness.

These qualities should form the foundation on which spiritual life should be built. Gopinathji viewed that one should not undertake any special exercises for awakening *kundalini*, the seven centres of man representing the divine consciousness, a trend which is commonly seen in the present era. *Kundalini*, the spiritual power lying dormant in man can be awakened by intense love for God.

Ramakrishna Paramahamsa held similar views when he said that love of God removes the veil of Maya to awaken *kundalini*. The well-known Vedantic teacher Swami Vivekananda proclaimed that selfless work done for the good of others awakens *kundalini*. Like all great spiritual leaders, Gopinathji said that there can be no spiritual progress as long as man is attached to worldly gains and has not given up worldly desires. For spiritual competency a man should also get rid of his ego by surrendering at the feet of God or Guru.

Gopinathji believed in the dictum—Silence is God. Like Ramana Maharishi, Gopinathji observed long spells of silence. He also believed both in knowledge and activity. He said that if there is a realized soul at work his influence will benefit not only his people but the entire world. Like Jesus Christ Gopinathji cured some dreaded diseases of his devotees and extended their lives.

Bhagavan Gopinathji is now widely known and is venerated across the globe. In recognition of his status as a global saint, Government of India issued a commemorative stamp during his birth centenary year in 1998. Those who worship Gopinathji are firm in their conviction that they can never return empty handed after offering prayers to him.

Sri Sri Ravi Shankar

Sri Sri Ravi Shankar, who is one of the world's most inspirational and dynamic spiritual leaders is the founder of the Art of Living Foundation which is spreading peace, love and human values to the entire global community. It has its branches in more than 140 countries. The Art of Living Foundation conducts short courses to restore human values and eliminate stress emphasizing on *sadhana* as well as *seva* or service. Sri Sri Ravi Shankar is also the founder of International Association for Human Values (IAHV). In his talks, Sri Sri Ravi Shankar lays emphasis on practical wisdom which touches both head and heart. The programmes conducted by the Art of Living lay emphasis on holistic development of body, mind and spirit.

Primarily, Sri Sri Ravi Shankar lays utmost stress on cheerfulness not only in terms of smile on lips but cheerfulness of heart. He says serving others is the expression of joy and love. Man must contribute to the well-being of all around him and to the whole world. All human beings can contribute as we all are born with many positive and good qualities and we must attempt to manifest them in our outer conduct.

Sri Sri Ravi Shankar says that first and foremost you are divine as God resides within all. God is not an object which is away from you. You are the wave and he is the ocean. To see God is an illusion because you are yourself Divine—*tat tvam asi.* World is one family—*vasudhaiva kutumbakam.* You may belong to any community, state or country but in reality you are a global citizen and therefore you should love one and all irrespective of caste, creed, nationality or sex. According to Sri Sri Ravi Shankar, enlightenment is going into the core of your self and living our life form there. We are born with silence and as we grow we lose our silence and start living with words mixed into our heads. We have to get back to heart getting back to silence and this is enlightenment. That is why it is said that longest journey is from head to heart and it must be completed if a person has to live delightfully.

Regarding negative karmas, Sri Sri Ravi Shankar says that spiritual practices and *satsang* burn their seeds. When you praise other, you take others' good karma and when you blame, you take on their bad karma. This is a big lesson for those who indulge in blame culture, very commonly seen in the society. Sri Sri Ravi Shankar further says that man must have faith in oneself, faith in the world and faith in the Divine. He calls faith as man's wealth.

A religious person is he who is righteous and loving, who cares for all. Religion should become all encompassing. Religion should end in spirituality to encompass all wisdom in the world. The ultimate purpose of life is to be of service to others. One must live in present because joy is never in tomorrow, it is always now. Sri Sri Ravi Shankar underscores that all religions and scriptures are true and they teach the same basic truth. We must respect all prophets and scriptures because there is commonality in them. Every major tradition or religion has made a contribution to wisdom. You may follow one faith but honour all other faiths and paths.

Sri Sri Ravi Shankar is a multi-facet humanitarian whose vision is to make the world violence and stress free. He emphasizes on love, cheerfulness, practical wisdom, service and harmony. He asks us to appreciate beauty which is always associated with shyness that softens the beauty. His advice to mankind is to give, share, help and love. He further advises to give preference to meditation and spiritual practices over material benefits. "Be peaceful within as peace proceeds happiness which is a prerequisite for enlightenment. Therefore identify what makes you happy. Be curious and do not expect everyone to agree with you." Regarding science and spirituality, Sri Sri Ravi Shankar says that deepening in mystery of creation is science and deepening in mystery of self is spirituality.

Regarding religion and politics, Sri Sri Ravi Shankar says that the role of religion is to make one righteous and loving, and politics means caring for people and their welfare. So, a religions person, who will be righteous and loving, will definitely look after the welfare of all, and thus he is a true politician. In the same light, a politician, who truly cares for the welfare of the people, will be righteous and loving and cannot but be religious. What a beautiful in-depth study of religion and politics which every politician in our country must realize and follow. Only then will the controversy over religions and politics disappear. For stress management, Sri Sri Ravi Shankar advises everyone to follow 4s—*Sadhna*, *Satsang*, *Seva* and Silence. Sri Sri Ravi Shankar calls life a celebration. He strongly exhorts everyone to celebrate life.

Sri Sathya Sai Baba

One of the living spiritual saints of the present time, Sri Sathya Sai Baba is working tirelessly for the revival of human values not only in India but also across the world. He is respected all over for his teachings of love and service. He founded Sri Sathya International Centre for human values at New Delhi in 1999 to conduct programmes for teaching human values. He is also the chancellor of Sai University, which teaches spiritual education to students. In addition, free medical treatment is provided in the hospitals run under the aegis of Sri Satya Sai Medical Trust.

Sri Sathya International Centre for human values conducts orientation programmes which covers subjects like self-actualization, leadership, character and human values. The programmes are conducted for school and college principals, teachers and students. The purpose of these programmes is to transfer all into men and women of character.

The thrust of the teaching of Sai Baba is that one should surrender to God. The moment you surrender your problems it become God's responsibilities. Surrender also kills man's ego. Love more and more people, love more and more intensely, transfer love into service and service into worship is the acme of Sai Baba's teachings.

He calls truth, sense control, equanimity, forbearance and

compassion the five life breaths which are inseparable from man for his higher journey. Sai Baba emphasizes on five basic values of life which are truth, non-violence, righteousness, love and peace. A person who practises these values and experiences joy therefrom, and shares this joy with others is called a leader. He says that human personality manifests fully when there is harmony and unity between body, mind and *atma*.

Sai Baba defines leadership as idealism in action. He says character is life, power and holiness. Without transforming character and packing the brain with information can only result in damaging the brain. Fill up the brain with high thoughts and highest ideals and place these ideals day and night before yourself and out of that will come a great work. Sai Baba's contribution in the education field is noteworthy.

Paramahamsa Yogananda

Paramahamsa Yoganandaji was born in India in 1893. He was the first great master of India who lived in the West for over 30 years. Recognized as a world prominent spiritual figure, he taught science of Yoga to the West. He founded Yogoda Satsang Society of India in 1917. In 1920, he formed a society called Self-realization Fellowship Society. Yoganandaji's famous work *Autobiography of a Yogi* has been published in 15 different languages. He had initiated over one lakh students in Yoga, a scientific technique for awakening divine consciousness in man. This technique was formed as Kriya Yoga. The other famous work of Yoganandaji is his commentary on the *Bhagavad Gita* called *God talks to Arjuna*. In a fitting tribute to Yoganandaji, the Government of India issued a commemorative stamp in his name in 1977.

Rabindranath Tagore

Popularly known as Gurudev Tagore, he was the founder of Visva Bharati Institute which imparts morality based education. Tagore was a spiritualist at the core but he also wrote poems, stories, novels, essays and dramas. He was equally interested in music and painting and his interest in the field of education was not less by any standard. Tagore was also a true environmentalist. He defined tree as a symbol of timeless patience. He believed in nationalism but only that nationalism which would lead to internationalism. His definition of patriotism is not only love for one's country but love for humanity. Tagore is also referred to as Tagore the feminist; feminism which was for equality of women with men and not labelling women as separate sex.

Saint Kabir

Born in the 15th Century, Kabir did not call himself a Hindu or a Muslim, yet he was loved by both Hindus and Muslims. Kabir was influenced by the *Upanishad*. He was a poet who composed his verses and songs in mixed language. In *Kabir Vani,* one gets the taste of a number of languages prevalent in India at his time. Kabir said that pure *bhakti* does not need ritualistic aid. Dip in holy water reinforces faith in God but dip in one's own self leads to knowledge of God or Real Self. Saints should do good to others. He compared saints to a tree which gives fruit to others without eating one's own fruit.

Mahatma Gandhi

Calling Gandhiji a saint is fully justified as he was totally spiritual at the core of his personality. He was a *karma yogi* in the true sense of the word. He was an extremely keen student of the *Bhagavad Gita* and demonstrated its teachings in his conduct. He once said that his supreme ambition of life was to wipe every tear from every eye. His gospel of non-violence puts him in the same rank as Buddha and Mahavira.

Gandhiji's views on religion and politics were simple and straightforward. In fact, he can be called a religious person in the guise of a politician. He said that religion is realization of truth and politics was a way to live in that truth:

"I could not be leading a religious life unless I identify myself with the whole of mankind and I could not do so unless I took part in politics."

Those who say that religion should not be mixed with politics are those who do not understand religion. Gandhiji called politics without morality a sin and politics without principles a deadly and dirty game. He said, "As long as I am alive, I will do politics in religion and religion in politics. Religion is like water to morality. Morality cannot be taught without teaching religion."

Gandhiji emphasized on single standard of conduct for both

public and private life. Human mind cannot be divided into water tight compartments called social, political and religious. He said that one's life should be like an open book. If you keep secrets, you can never speak truth. To Gandhiji, non-violence is the highest form of courage. To him, deeper meaning of non-violence meant accepting other ideas and not thrusting own preferences down the throat of others.

I feel bad when I see people showing utmost reverence to Gandhiji but not in the least showing any concern or regard for his teachings. Our political system must accept the advice of Gandhiji on politics and make it a clean game. For how long we can neglect Gandhiji's teachings on the pleas that India is a secular state? In the name of secularism, we have totally eliminated our spiritual and moral teachings, which is not good for our country. Gandhiji called literacy as the beginning of education and highest aim of education is knowledge of God. Education should contribute towards development of head, heart and hands.

> *Faith is to believe what you do not see; the reward of this faith is to see what you believe.*
>
> ***Saint Augustine***

Leadership, Character and Success

Take up one idea. Make that one idea our life—think of it, dream of it, live on that idea. Let the brain, muscles, nerves, every part of your body, be full of that idea, and just leave every other idea alone. This is the way to success.

Swami Vivekananda

Leadership

Leadership can be defined in a number of ways. One authentic definition of leadership was formed during World War I. It states: "Leadership is the capacity to frame plans that will succeed and the faculty to persuade others to carry them out in the face of all difficulties—even death." Leader is one who has courage. There is another definition of leadership which says that a leader is one who generates new ideas.

Sri Sathya Sai Baba defines leadership as idealism in action. According to him, true leader is one who is dedicated to the welfare of all and who upholds the reputation of country. Leader is one who marches ahead. He who practises truth, non-violence, righteousness, love and peace is a true leader. He is also a leader who possesses spirit of sacrifice and holds himself as an ideal for human beings. A leader is also one who does not panic but achieves the goal uncompromisingly.

One definition of leader is that who knows every inch of ground and does not believe in short cuts. Short cuts may make life easy but can also put you on wrong route. It is for this reason that wise people do not opt for short cuts in life.

Leadership is most infectious. There is a Persian saying that if the king plucks one apple, people will take away roots.

The *Bhagavad Gita* says that whatever great men do ordinary people follow. Whatever goal they set, people try to achieve it. Great men are path setters. Does it mean that great men are leaders? It can also mean that leaders are great men. It is said that some are born great, some achieve greatness and some have greatness thrust upon them.

Personally, I value that leader who achieves greatness by his sincerity and his unaided efforts. Because one who achieves greatness on his own has travelled every inch of the ground to reach the top position. For him, greatness is self-made. Such leader shows abundance of self-belief. Even those who are born great or who have greatness thrust upon them can become great leaders in the true sense with self-effort and personal example, without depending much on the circumstances that have made them great.

Leadership is a state and not a status. It is a state when we handle situations and take responsibility. More responsibility more power. Leadership is a state of personal growth based on self-transformation. A leader should be humanist. It is through humanism when a leader can feel the sufferings of others. Some of the qualities of good leader are selflessness which is the foundation of leadership, saneness in words, thoughts and deeds, transparency and non-duplicity. Good leaders are good managers as well. They are good in self-management. They have the ability to include others in their vision. Good leaders deal with others effectively. Effective dealing constitutes as high as nearly 90 per cent of leadership qualities. Good leaders are men of character and they influence others with personal examples. Leader is one who defeats problems and shows receptivity to new ideas.

Character

Character is greater than career. Character is the distinctive mark of all great men and is the life force of a person. It is measured in terms of moral strength and righteousness of the individual. Where there is righteousness at heart, there is beauty in character, says Chinese philosopher Confucius. Dr Radhakrishnan says that countries are made great not by anything else but by ordinary men of character who have a sense of purpose, are loyal and are ready to suffer for the sake of upward progress towards building a better life.

Character is important not only for youth but also for all age groups, including those who are controlling the affairs of our country. Character and discipline are deeply interconnected. A person of character is highly disciplined and a highly disciplined person is a man of character. Character qualities are inwardly.

It is an inner movement anchored on morality. Without ethical foundation, character cannot be formed. It may be good to conquer external nature but it is greater to conquer inner nature. It is good to know the laws that govern stars and planets but it is greater to know the laws that govern our passion and feelings. Character is the backbone of a person, and if it is not good, the man is labelled as morally corrupt.

Swami Vivekananda says if you want to judge the character of a man, look not at his great performance but watch him to do his most common action. Even fools may become hero at one time or the other. Swami Vivekananda further says that Indian ideal of religion is the highest ideal for building national character which is made up of the character of people living in the country, their religion and the government that is keenly interested in the people of the state. A man of character feels unity with all. He is a treat to watch as he does all actions sincerely. He realizes the sufferings of mankind and desires to reduce them in whatever way he can. Character is the sum total of impressions in the mind of a person and these impressions are based on his habits which are related to his repeated actions.

Without ethic foundation, character cannot be formed as it is based on inner movement anchored on morality. A person of character has an urge to live for others. He is energetic by nature. Spiritual life without character building is like making a house without a cementing agent.

For character building, human beings are to be humanized, morally uplifted and spiritually awakened. All this requires self-awareness to know where we stand. We have to bring about positive changes in our attitude towards life. Man's attitude plays an important role in character formation. We have to become open hearted and broad minded. We have to acquire purity of heart. Value-based education sows seeds of morality, selflessness, purity and simplicity. We have to develop honesty and integrity while dealing with others. Integrity means doing right things even if no one is watching. Character is the sum total of person's values, beliefs and personality.

Success

Success literally means attainment of one's goal. No one meaning of success is same for two different people. For a sportsman, success means winning a medal. For a worldly man, success means doing well in his job or business which secures comforts and luxuries for him. For a writer, success means his writings being appreciated by one and all; for a student, success means securing a high grade in exams, and for a housewife, success means looking after the needs of all members of family and commanding their respects. All these definitions of success are partial and not complete.

Swami Vivekananda says that being successful in life means performing all activities as a service to God for benefiting human kind. Successful people are those who serve fellow beings. He considers successful person as one who lives for others with love. They are successful who spend time in serving others for the benefit of the world at large.

So what is real success? Definition of true success is to remain dedicated to a cause which is greater than one's self. Real success is more inclined to man's duty towards his fellow beings rather than looking after himself exclusively. Real success is complete inner growth which is your lifetime constant companion, and which will never leave you even when you face adverse circumstances. Worldly success might be with us today but may not remain with us tomorrow. But this does not mean that worldly success has to be discredited. Worldly success is equally important but it has to be supplemented with inner growth and success. Worldly success and inner success go hand in hand with inner growth monitoring the worldly success. Worldly success is to be supplemented with inner growth.

To be successful in life means to have a constant urge to evolve oneself to a higher state of existence. To be successful means to become a part of world development process. Sri Sri Ravi Shankar says that what holds the key to success is awareness, sense of belongingness and commitment. Awareness means being conscious, interested in knowing, informed and not ignorant. Sense of belongingness means I belong to you and not that you belong to me. When you say that you belong to me, there is a sense of possessiveness, but when you say that I belong to you, there is no such feeling. You can belong to the whole world without a sense of possession. As they say, make the whole world your own.

Commitment means being fully involved with anything you undertake. Commitment means giving one hundred per cent to anything that you do. To be successful one should be free from all forms of limitations; one should be living in the present moment.

To be successful means you are useful to people. To be successful means you love everyone around you. Without ethical foundation, none can achieve success inwardly, which is the main component of personality development. For a successful person, whole life is a process of giving. He always gives more than what he takes from others. He believes in the power of love, and to him, happiness is the key to success.

Success is an inner state. It is a feeling of inner worth which is higher than worldly success. Success ultimately lies in gaining knowledge about one's own self. To be real successful is to be a man of values.

Einstein says, "Try not to become a man of success but a man of values." If you are successful in worldly affairs but you are not morally upright, then you are not successful in the real sense. Real success lies in our sincerity, honesty, transparency and, most importantly, in our attitude towards life. Attitude is the inner waking of mind which is a vital factor in achieving success. Finally, real success lies in refining and elevating our thoughts so that our thinking becomes positive. This also indicates that secret of success lies within us.

Conclusion

In the end, I again come back to the theme of the book—'Success is No Fluke'. As stated in the contents, to be successful we have to develop our personality on spiritual foundation. When we do that, we overcome hypocrisy, double standards and pretensions. Then we remain what we are. So, the first requirement to develop a personality is to Be Yourself. It is also true that when we are doing well in worldly life, our mind may not get inclined towards higher values of life or to understand what is ethics and spirituality. Here, we have to realize that even with outer success, we have to become a spiritually-inclined person. As the *Bhagavad Gita* says that where there is a marriage between worldly and spiritual lives, there are sure fortune victory, prosperity and statesmanship.

The other thing I wish to mention is that as parents, it is our duty to bring up our children in such a way that they become responsible citizens of our country. Mother is the first teacher of child, father the second, school teacher the third and God the final and ultimate teacher—*Krishnam vande jagat gurum*. So, as parents, we have to understand and practise various aspects of spirituality and personality development even if we feel there is no need for us to do so. We can only teach what we know well; all the more reason for us to learn it for the sake of children.

We also take up to spirituality or turn to God when we face worldly problems. This is true for many of us. In the *Bhagavad Gita*, Arjuna turned to God when he was totally depressed on being faced to fight his kith and kin. Lord Krishna taught him how to overcome his grief which is clearly evident when at the end of the *Bhagavad Gita,* Arjuna says, "I will discharge my duties," which in his case was fighting the Kurukshetra battle.

Finally, I am reminded of what Kunti, the mother of Pandavas says, "Oh God, always beset me with problems in life so that I never forget you."

When a man develops his personality fully, he accepts that no one can harm him except he himself. Then he realizes that people would behave with him as he decides. Then he understands that it is he who will attract good or bad people towards him. He also understands that it is he who makes himself sad or bright and not the circumstances outside. A developed personality will always look for his responsibilities and not his rights. He will never react to what others think of him.

> *Instead of saying that man is the creature of circumstance, it would be nearer the mark to say that man is the architect of circumstance.*
>
> ***Thomas Carlyle***

Postscript
Spirituality and Soldier

In the Army, people from different religions and castes come together and live as one family. They identify themselves with the Indian concept of the world being a part of the extended family. This comes not at the cost of neglecting one or the other religion. Religious festivals of all faiths are celebrated with great enthusiasm and fervour. A soldier may belong to any faith, yet he honours all other faiths. When an Army unit goes into war against enemy, all members of the unit invoke the motherland or a common deity before actual assault. For example, *Bharat Mata Ki Jai* is the battle cry of an Army unit before it is launched against the enemy.

What motivates a soldier to give his best at the risk of his own life is his love for the motherland. To defend his country is his duty as well as religion. He is sincerely committed to his duty which in this case is protection of his motherland at all cost. In the *Mahabharata,* it is stated that only two types can pierce the constellation of Sun and reach *Brahman*—a *sanyasi* steeped into Yoga and a warrior who falls in the battlefield. The *Bhagavad Gita* records that when a soldier dies in battle, he attains heaven which is the highest good. A soldier is highly disciplined, sincere and wedded to his duty. Before a soldier is launched into action, he acquires a clear understanding that victory shall be his. This is what Guru Gobind Singh said, "*Nischay Kar Apni Jeet Karo*".

A soldier's biggest quality is obedience of orders and this is what makes him disciplined. Greek philosopher Aristotle pointed out that one who has never learned to obey cannot be a good commander. A soldier accepts responsibility spontaneously, truly justifying that one's duty stands at the highest pedestal. His motto is 'Service Before Self'. He takes pride in performing his duties for the sake of his country.

The values that are taught in the Army are spiritual in nature. The Army officers are graded on the basis of certain values referred to as Officers Like Qualities (OLQs). Briefly, these qualities are—cooperation with all, courage to face complex situations, strong will power, intelligence or reasoning ability, the ability to adjust to the requirement of a particular situation, ability to sacrifice personal gain for a higher cause, cheerfulness and liveliness under strenuous conditions and taking pride in the organization one belongs to called Espirit De Corps. These qualities match with the divine qualities enumerated in the *Bhagavad Gita,* specially the quality of working selflessly and adventurously.

I am of the strong view that ex-servicemen should be employed for promoting higher values of life in the society. They are very well equipped to do so and are ideally suited to serve the country even after retirement. India should take pride in a soldier.